ADHD
WORKS
At Work

ADHD WORKS
At Work

Leanne Maskell

Cover design by Ellie Perkins @ Write & Sunny
Design and typesetting by Danny Lyle

For Beth Lewis - thank you for making
ADHD Works work with me.

Foreword

Neurodiversity at work is not just about supporting neurodivergent people. It is also about creating a better workplace for everyone, regardless of how they wish to describe themselves. When we create workplaces that are inclusive of neurodiversity, we create workplaces that are more innovative and productive by embracing diversity and all the advantages it offers.

As a Neurodiversity Advocacy Lead at Google, I am committed to creating a workplace where everyone feels they belong, because only when you feel you belong can you thrive. As such, I am grateful for the opportunity to write this foreword for Leanne's book, as this book provides such a great resource of information for anyone interested in tapping into the benefits of neurodiversity. Only when we understand each other's strengths and struggles, can we create an environment where everyone dares to surpass expectations.

When I was 42 years old, I was diagnosed with ADHD. Finally, I was able to understand why I did things differently in the workplace. Instead of feeling as if I didn't fit in, I began to appreciate the benefit of not conforming. The diagnosis was a blessing in disguise, as I began to finally appreciate how ADHD allowed me to tackle problems in non-conventional ways.

It has been exactly 5 years since I have disclosed my ADHD at work. I am very conscious, and fortunate, that I have had a very positive experience regarding the support provided by my colleagues and managers.

Leanne provides a timely and very comprehensive contribution to the conversation about ADHD in the workplace. Many situations that Leanne describes were very recognisable to me. I wish this book was given to me as a roadmap after my diagnosis, as this would have given me more confidence in knowing that neurodiversity truly is a blessing.

This book is essential reading for anyone who wants to understand neurodiversity, especially from an ADHD perspective, and its implications in the workplace. It is a valuable resource for employers, managers, HR professionals, and employees alike who are committed to creating a more inclusive and equitable workforce.

When neurodivergent people are able to thrive in the workplace, everyone benefits!

Lisette Schipper
Neurodiversity Advocacy Lead, Google

Contents

Introduction

Finding out you've got ADHD as an adult is like being told you're a wizard with magical powers - but unlike Harry Potter, you've still got to go to work.

The psychiatrists don't give you your invitation to Hogwarts. They don't explain what ADHD is or what it means to be neurodivergent. You're not told that this could be a disability, or how to navigate this identity-crisis. They might give you some medication, but there's no instruction manual explaining how this will *literally change the way you think*.

No one explains to you how to act normal after finding out that you aren't normal. It might leave you questioning everything you've ever known or thought about yourself, including all of your life decisions until this point.

I know this, because I've lived it - and as an ADHD Coach, I support others through this on a daily basis. As the Founder of ADHD Works, I also train employers to do the same.

Being diagnosed with ADHD enabled me to get and keep a 'real' job for over 2 years: one of my greatest achievements of all time. Having medical confirmation that my brain was indeed likely to quit again meant I concocted elaborate traps for myself, such as living over the road from my office as an attempt to force myself to stay. There was no relatable information about ADHD on the internet, no social media vortexes, and *definitely* no one talking about it on LinkedIn, of all places.

It was only from working in mental health and disability law that I learned that I didn't have to bear this burden by myself. Understanding that ADHD could be a disability, and I wouldn't be fired for having a brain that worked differently to 'most' people, meant I could relax and be myself.

Most people are not so fortunate, which is what led me to set up ADHD Works.

ADHD has only been diagnosed in adults since 2008 in the UK, which means that potentially millions of people have lived their entire adult lives with no idea that they are neurodivergent. They may have spent years struggling to be 'normal', beating themselves up for being lazy or stupid when they are simply different.

ADHD is diagnosed from a deficit model, meaning that it's typically diagnosed when a person's life has reached a certain level of disorder as a result of this neurodevelopmental condition. This doesn't mean that the *person* with ADHD is disordered, or that there's anything wrong with them: it's society that sets these standards.

However, this is reflected in the workplace, where as adults we are typically expected to spend the majority our lives, literally using our brain to 'make a living'. The different ways of thinking that accompany being neurodivergent are a huge asset for work, but they can also be a disability, coming at a huge cost to the individual.

Employers are now catching up, chasing the unique innovation and creativity of minds that literally think outside the box - but this box is usually of their own making. ADHD doesn't fit into the 'traditional 'professional' mould. I act before I think, chase my creative ideas, and figure the rest out later. I work backwards. I go from A to Z, instead of following instructions for the sake of following instructions. I can go and train some of the biggest companies in the world, like Disney, Deutsche Bank and Microsoft, but I probably wouldn't be able to sit down long enough to write a cover letter for a 'normal' job application at any of these places.

Why I wrote this book

As the Founder of ADHD Works, I've been fortunate enough to work with hundreds of people and their employers, all navigating the same challenges around

ADHD at work. These challenges could be very easily solved, but there's a lot of fear - on both sides.

Talking about ADHD at work can be tough. So this book is my attempt at making that process a little less scary for everyone, making the medical and legal jargon a little more human and accessible.

It's a guide to making ADHD work at work for employers and employees, so they can enjoy the endless benefits of an inclusive and accessible workplace. There's templates and exercises throughout the book, helping you to put it into practice, which you can adjust as you'd like to.

Ultimately, this book was created to bridge the gap between understanding, supporting, and harnessing ADHD at work, which is how it's structured:

Firstly, we need to 'name it to tame it'

It's important to have an 'ADHD lens' when navigating ADHD at work, understanding what it is and how it can show up for an individual. If you've met one person with ADHD, you've met one person with ADHD!

We'll look at ADHD from the perspective of differences in executive functioning skills, whilst breaking down highly sensitive concepts like 'disability' and 'neurodiversity' in chapters 1 and 2. It's important to do this in a legal context, because it's impossible to use your rights if you don't know what they are.

In the UK, the Equality Act protects people with disabilities against discrimination within society, including at work, which includes people with ADHD who meet this criteria. Although it's hoped that employers would support everybody that works with them, especially those who are disadvantaged through no fault of their own, this isn't always what happens in reality. This isn't necessarily because they don't want to, but because the law can be a bit confusing to apply on an individual basis.

This is because employers have a legal duty to **pro-actively do something** by making reasonable adjustments. These are essentially changes to the way things are done at work for disabled people, which will be different for everybody. In chapter 3, we'll look at how to talk about ADHD at work to ensure that everybody is on the same page.

Secondly, we need to 'level the playing field'

To support people with ADHD at work, employers should have an inclusive and accessible culture, so we'll look at how to turn awareness into action in chapter 4.

In chapter 5, we'll look at reasonable adjustments that help people with ADHD at work. These are legally required to put disabled people on a level playing field with their non-disabled colleagues. In the context of ADHD, reasonable adjustments exist to help us do our job like everybody who doesn't have ADHD is able to.

However, implementing these can be very challenging to navigate, especially if a disabled person doesn't know what support they need to help them. When we're diagnosed with ADHD, we're not given a handy breakdown of strategies that work for us - we're just left to figure this out by ourselves, which is what this chapter is designed to help with.

This is likely to happen after a lifetime of struggles, and it can be very difficult to untangle this and ask for help, because we may not even be able to imagine anything different to what we know. Having supportive cultures, policies, and training in place enables everybody to figure this out together, instead of retreating in fear.

In chapter 6, we'll explore how to navigate the UK Government's Access to Work scheme, which can help to pay for support above and beyond adjustments, with awards available of up to tens of thousands of pounds per year.

Without proper support in place, significant challenges and conflicts can arise around ADHD at work, such as in relation to performance, which we'll explain how to manage in chapter 7.

Ultimately, supporting people with ADHD effectively at work means that we have the same opportunities as our peers to contribute all of our efforts to our job, instead of wasting energy masking who we are.

Thirdly, we can thrive with ADHD - not just survive!

Having a workplace where we feel able to be ourselves allows everybody to harness the unique benefits and strengths that have been scientifically proven to accompany ADHD, which are covered in chapter 8.

In chapter 9, we'll cover specific ADHD coaching skills to empower employees to provide support tailored towards ADHD brains, helping people to move forward and embrace their ADHD at work.

As we have have interest-led brains, we'll cover the best management styles that work for ADHD brains in chapter 10, before understanding how to cultivate the best long-term performance and progression for employees with ADHD to thrive in their careers in chapter 11.

I've had the privilege of coaching and working with hundreds of people with ADHD, and every single one of them has blown me away with their passion, intelligence, strength, and compassion. Many have experienced similar struggles to me in the workplace, where it's easy to feel as though there is something 'wrong' with us for being different.

This book is a reminder that being different is a brilliant and beautiful thing - in and out of the world of work. I strongly believe that our society needs neurodivergent brains to move forward, because we can't solve problems with the same thinking that created them. Our world is zooming forward at super fast speed, and it needs similarly whizzy brains that can keep up with this rate of constant change.

ADHD brains don't just keep up: we thrive on chaos. We're excellent in a crisis, thrive under pressure, and think outside the box by definition. We're the hyper-active hunters in a world where we've become conditioned to see 'normality' as sitting in front of a screen for 7 hours a day. The Covid-19 pandemic blasted neuronormative standards apart, showing that it is not necessary for people to commute for hours to a certain desk to look into their laptops to be able to do their job.

As our society moves beyond the box it has created for itself, it's time for the hunters to shine.

How to read this book

I wrote this book to support the understanding, support and harnessing of ADHD at work, using a format that I hope will enable it to be picked up and read in any way that feels relevant to an employer, an employee or a potential employee. Although the book is mainly focused on ADHD within UK employment, I hope the underlying principles discussed are relevant to anybody interested in the topic.

There are templates and exercises included throughout the book which you might find helpful to use, share or adapt as works best for you, or someone you know.

This book isn't aimed at one type of person: it's for employees and employers alike. It's intended to bridge the gap of communication, as a resource for ADHD at work. However, it should not be relied upon as legal or medical advice. Everybody's situation will be unique to them, and you should always seek expert support where needed.

I've tried my best to make complex and vague concepts accessible and engaging, but please remember that I am just one person with ADHD. What I share in this book is based on my personal knowledge and experiences, but it might look very different for somebody else.

I've tried to make this book as inclusive as possible, whilst focusing primarily on the legal context of disability and ADHD in the UK, but it's important to remember that language is a highly sensitive and personal topic. The wishes of an individual should always be respected and prioritised, especially when it comes to language surrounding disability and conditions like ADHD.

This book exists because I recognise my privilege and unusual position as a person with ADHD who has had a range of experiences navigating ADHD at work, who has a legal background in mental health and disability legal policy, and who has worked extensively to coach those with ADHD as well as to train many other ADHD coaches. This book shares some of the knowledge and experience I have acquired. I hope it will help contribute towards a future world where ADHD is fully supported and embraced within the workplace.

That having been said, it is important to remember the reality of social and health inequities that contribute to ongoing barriers for inclusion in our society as reflected within the workplace, such as race - which are also critical to address.

Please approach this book with an open mind: my intention is to foster constructive conversations around important subjects, which often do not take place out of a fear of 'getting things wrong'.

There's no right or wrong way to read this book - I just hope you like it.

Please feel free to contact me at www.adhdworks. info to access coaching, training, resources or anything else that I can help with - I'd love to hear from you!

Understanding ADHD

Chapter 1
Disability vs Diversity

What is neurodiversity?

Neurodiversity refers to the differences between all human minds, as everybody exists, feels, thinks, acts, processes and functions differently. In the last few years, the term has become very popular when referring to neurodevelopmental conditions like ADHD and Autism, but it's very fast-moving.

So although we **all** think differently from one another, there are certain standards which we could refer to as 'neuronormative' - essentially, what our society calls 'normal' ways of being. We're subject to these expectations right from birth, with society dictating what should be 'normal' in terms of development and skills in relation to age, such as the ability to walk or talk.

Think of exams such as GCSEs and A Levels. Our society has decided the criteria that we all 'should' be learning and able to achieve, with top marks reserved for people who can meet these criteria in a certain way (i.e by sitting in school for a number of hours per day). These marks can go on to shape our career prospects and future, which are further subject to neurotypical expectations, such as the requirement to work from an office for 8 hours a day.

Our ancestors would have had very different neuronormative standards, as they'd be out catching food and running around - no screens to be seen! When we talk about ADHD, it's easy to think of the hyperactive, naughty schoolboy disrupting the class - as opposed to questioning whether it's natural for children to sit still and listen in silence for 7 hours per day, 5 days a week.

An individual whose functioning falls within the dominant neuronormative standards of thinking and acting can be referred to as 'neurotypical'. For example, 'most' people in my class who were able to listen to the teacher might have been neuro-typical. In contrast, I was neurodivergent, because I couldn't listen to more than 1 word without my mind wandering off into a different dimension, only reappearing at the end, when I'd realised I hadn't processed a single word that had been said over the last hour.

To use this example, I'm neurodivergent because I'm an individual whose mind and functioning falls outside of these neuronormative standards. As a group, our class would have been *neurodiverse*, because we'd all have our own unique brains and ways of thinking. There are many different ways a person can be neurodivergent, including Autism, Dyslexia, Dyspraxia and Dyscalculia, to name a few.

Is being neurodivergent a superpower?

As ADHD is a neurodevelopmental condition, this means that those with it literally think differently to 'most' people. We have a different operating system. Imagine that neurotypical people have Google Chrome brains, and my ADHD brain is an Apple MacBook. If you put the instructions for a Chrome into my brain, it won't respond in the same way as most people - it'll find its own unique way of process-ing these instructions, or it might not work at all.

It's not that one way of operating is necessarily better or worse than another, but that they are simply different. For example, I managed to get a law degree by hyper-focusing at the end of the year, instead of going to lectures and studying like every-body else throughout. This could be seen as positive in meaning I saved a huge amount of time, for example, but also negative in the fact that I graduat-ed feeling as though it was a waste of my money and time - not to mention, with huge imposter syndrome! However, it's easy to see how this could be seen as a 'superpower' in our society that happens to hold law degrees up on intellectual pedestals.

In contrast, ADHD severely disables other areas of my life. I might be able to write a book, but I seriously struggle to look after myself with the basics, such as showering, eating, getting dressed, washing my clothes, changing my bedsheets, socialising with other people, managing my energy, and so on.

It's important to be mindful of this when talking about neurodiversity, as it can be a highly sensitive and individual topic. ADHD is only diagnosed when symptoms 'disorder' a person's life, which means that those who don't experience the severe challenges associated with it, may not necessarily find out they have ADHD. For example, a friend of mine is an energy healer and yoga teacher, who displays all of the brilliant strengths associated with ADHD such as creativity and curiosity. However, she would be very unlikely to be diagnosed as she doesn't hold herself to neuronormative expectations, as she works completely according to her own schedule and standards. If she tried to work in an office, this would likely be a very different story!

Harnessing neurodiversity and setting people up with environments where they can thrive and utilise their unique strengths and ways of thinking is extremely important for our society. This applies for everybody, but especially neurodivergent people who may be 'disabled' by society as a result of these neuronormative standards.

Is ADHD a disability?

There are several different models of disability, but for the purposes of this book, disability is referred to in the context of the Equality Act 2010, which protects disabled people from discrimination in our society at large, including within the workplace. It's important to check with someone about how they feel about this language, as disability can be a highly charged concept and everybody will feel differently. However, we are looking at it in a purely legal sense, including what this means for a workplace.

Under section 6 of the the Equality Act 2010, a person is disabled if they have a physical or mental impairment that has a 'substantial' ('more than minor or trivial') and 'long-term' (12 months or more, or is expected to persist for that long) negative effect on their ability to do normal day to day activities.[1]

Some conditions are automatically covered when they're diagnosed, such as cancer, but many are not, such as ADHD.

This being said, the diagnostic criteria for ADHD requires symptoms of hyperactivity, impulsivity, and/or inattention to cause at least moderate 'pervasive' negative impairment in two or more

---

1   https://www.gov.uk/definition-of-disability-under-equality-act-2010

'important settings' of a person's life, including social, familial, educational, and/or occupational settings.[2]

Ultimately, whether a condition qualifies as a disability or not under the Act depends on the individual circumstances of each person. If you've met one person with ADHD, you've met one person with ADHD! It's also a highly situational, lifelong condition, and some daily activities may be impacted far more than others.

If a workplace requires us to meet certain standards such as working 5 days a week from an office during specified hours to meet specified targets or expectations, it's likely that our ADHD may impact our ability to meet these standards in one way or another. ADHD literally relates to how a person thinks and acts, so it affects all areas of our life.

There are several day to day activities that take me much longer than my peers because of having ADHD, largely those involving executive functioning skills. For example, I struggle with seemingly 'easy' tasks such as administration and data entry much more than traditionally 'harder' tasks like research and writing reports, because of my ADHD. I wouldn't be able to do any of my work without someone to

2 https://www.nice.org.uk/guidance/ng87/resources/attention-deficit-hyperactivity-disorder-diagnosis-and-management-pdf-1837699732933

help me with this, because I'd be spending all of my time struggling with setting up zoom calls and trying to find missing information!

My ADHD means that I also struggle significantly with 'normal' activities outside of work, such as showering, cooking, and getting dressed, which can take me a lot longer (and much more effort!) than my peers. This has a cumulative impact on my work also, as this impacts my overall health and wellbeing.

This is a legal test, not a medical one. This is important because years long NHS waiting lists for ADHD assessments mean that many people may be protected under the Equality Act against discrimination because of their disability, despite not having a formal diagnosis. My ADHD disabled me before I had a formal diagnosis - I just didn't know it! So, if you're on a waiting list for ADHD and struggling at work, you are still fully deserving of that support. If you're struggling, you're struggling - and this is valid in itself.

Only the employment tribunal can rule on whether a person is disabled or not, which is where medical evidence such as a diagnosis may be required, but is not essential. This should be a final resort - although the employment tribunal process is free, obtaining legal advice and representation can be extremely expensive and difficult to access. Damages for disability discrimination are uncapped, which means that it's in an employer's best interest to believe people when they tell them they are disabled!

A person may be referred to an independent expert such as Occupational Health to help establish this and the support that could be put into place for an individual at work, but this is just their opinion. It's important that any referrals are followed up with appropriate conversations and action internally - this shouldn't be a checkbox.

Being disabled under the Equality Act doesn't mean that a person can't do their job. It simply means that they may face certain barriers in being able to do so in the same way as people who do not have this disability. The point of the law is to accommodate everybody, 'levelling up' the playing field for fairness and inclusion - which allows everybody to thrive as they are whilst contributing and participating in our society. Diversity benefits everybody, because there's no one 'right' way of doing things - we all have our unique strengths and challenges, which complement and support each other as a collective.

What happens if someone is disabled at work?

The Equality Act places a legal duty on employers and organisations to ensure that disabled people can access jobs, education, and services as easily as non-disabled people. This includes potential applicants of jobs, in addition to current employees.

This law also protects people with disabilities from a range of different types of discrimination. The focus of this book is on reasonable adjustments and hopefully having things in place so that discrimination doesn't arise, but as a very brief overview, these include:

- **Direct disability discrimination:** where a disabled person is treated worse because of their disability than a comparator, typically a non-disabled person who shares the same circumstances.

  For example, being put on a performance review because of symptoms directly relating to ADHD, such as impulsivity and time management. It's important that an employer knows or ought to have known about a disability for this to amount to discrimination.

- **Discrimination arising from disability:** where an employer treats someone negatively because of something arising from their disability, unless this can be objectively justified with sufficient reason and demonstration that this is proportionate - essentially, that they had no other choice.

  For example, this could look like being fired because of absences from work due to sickness, with no adjustments in place to accommodate this because of your disability. People with ADHD may need more absences from work than a non-disabled person because of their ADHD and need to attend medical appointments or co-morbidities, such as burnout.

- **Indirect disability discrimination:** it's unlawful for employers to apply a provision, criteria, or practice ('PCP') in a way that has a worse impact on disabled people compared to non-disabled people. However, this could be objectively justified with proportionate reasoning as above, if relevant.

  For example, this could look like awarding bonuses depending on people working from the office, with no adjustments made to accommodate this policy for those people who may not be able to work in an office due to their disability. People with ADHD may struggle with working in an office full time because of executive functioning challenges such as organisation and self-awareness, such as by becoming easily distracted by people talking around them or struggling with commuting.

- **Harassment related to disability:** it is unlawful for employers to act in a way in relation to a person's disability which creates a hostile or intimidating environment, or violates a person's dignity. Employers must also do what is reasonable to protect individuals from this kind of harass- ment from their colleagues (which would often be found to be acts of an employer). Essentially, environments must not be created or tolerated at work where a disabled person may be subject to unwanted, offensive, or exploitative behaviour in relation to their disability.

For example, this could look like people making derogatory comments about a colleague with ADHD or people with ADHD, such as by saying 'ADHD isn't real - get over it!'. Another example could be colleagues telling others about your disability in a way that violates your dignity. If you feel harassed, you are harassed.

- **Victimisation:** it's unlawful for employers to retal- iate or treat a person differently because they have complained about disability discrimination or helped others to do so, or may do so. Any behaviour related to the Equality Act is generally deemed a 'protected act'.

  For example, this may look like an employee who raises concerns about how their employer treats disabled people at work, such as by having no disability policy in place, being marginalised as a result.

- **Failure to make reasonable adjustments:** where an employer has breached their legal duty under the Equality Act to ensure workers and applicants are not substantially disadvantaged in carrying out or applying for a job because of a disability, in comparison to people who do not have a disability.

  They have a legal duty to make 'reasonable adjustments' which are changes deliberately designed to remove or reduce any barriers an individual may be faced with in doing or applying for a job because of a physical feature in the workplace premises, a failure to provide an 'auxiliary aid' such as extra equipment, or a provision, criterion or practice applied in the workplace, such as working arrangements.

The duty to make reasonable adjustments for people with ADHD at work is the main focus of this book, as this area of law can be challenging to get right. For example, adjustments must be 'reasonable' to apply in the circumstances, which are situation dependent, such as by consideration of an employers' resources and size, costs involved, impact on others / the business, and whether the adjustments have the prospect of being effective.

An example of this could look like an employee asking for an adjustment to work from home due to their ADHD. An outright denial of this with no reasoning provided may be found to be a failure to make reasonable adjustments, particularly if an employee was able to work from home previously, such as during the pandemic.

A common example I see is people requesting interview questions in advance due to their ADHD challenges associated with planning and anxiety around interviews. To deny this could be found to be a failure to make reasonable adjustments, especially given the ease with which this could be done!

Employment tribunal claims relating to neuro-diverse conditions and disability discrimination rose by 30% in one year, showing how serious it can be for employers to get this wrong.[3] Compensation awards are uncapped, meaning it can be very expensive for employers to break this law, with over £2.5 million awarded in one disability discrimination case.[4]

It's worth noting that this level of payout is very rare - in 2021/22, the average award for a disability discrimination case was £26,172.[5]

---

3   https://www.foxlawyers.com/employment-tribunal-claims-relating-to-neurodiversity-discrimination-jump-by-a-third-in-past-year/
4   Barrow v Kellog Brown and Root (UK) Ltd: 2303683/2018
5   https://www.dacbeachcroft.com/en/gb/articles/2023/january/employment-tribunals-statistics-published/

Template: Reasonable Adjustments Policy

In an ideal world, employers would have a policy in place that breaks down concepts such as disability, neurodiversity, and reasonable adjustments. Making this accessible to everybody enables everyone to access the support they need as needed, and setting out processes to be followed by employees ensures that everybody is on the same page - literally!

If your organisation doesn't have one, feel free to use this template below for inspiration, or head to www.adhdworks.info to access a free digital version.

1 Purpose

1.1 This policy explains how to access support in relation to a health condition that impacts a person at work, amounting to a disability under the Equality Act 2010. It aims to ensure every individual is supported in relation to their specific needs and is treated with confidentiality and dignity.

1.2 Under the Equality Act, a person is disabled if they have a 'physical or mental impairment that has a 'substantial' and 'long-term' negative effect on their ability to do normal daily activities.

1.3 We strongly promote diversity and inclusion, and value people feeling confident in being accepted and supported as they are at work.

1.4   Other relevant policies may include [e.g sickness absence policy, recruitment policies...]

2 Disclosure

2.1   Disclosure is the process of a person making a current or prospective employer aware of their disability and the impact it has on them. Disclosure is a personal, voluntary decision and will be treated confidentially. The purpose of disclosure is to ensure a person can be supported as effectively as possible at work, and they should never be treated negatively as a result.

2.2   To disclose a disability, a person should inform their line manager or other relevant identified employee about their health condition that they feel impacts them at work. This can be done via conversation or in writing but should be recorded and notified to Human Resources ('HR'), where applicable.

2.3   Upon disclosure, the person should be signposted to this policy and the Government's Access to Work scheme, which can help identify and pay for support. A follow up discussion about how they can be best supported should be arranged as soon as possible, as set out below.

2.4   The person's manager (or other relevant employee, such as an interviewer) should be offered training on how to best support a person with this condition, if available. They should feel confident in applying reasonable adjustments, how to access further support and be aware of the need to anticipate and/or offer potential adjustments that may be necessary as set out below.

3 Reasonable Adjustments

3.1   A reasonable adjustment is a change made to remove or reduce a disadvantage related to an employee's disability when doing a job, or a job applicant's disability when applying for a job. Reasonable adjustments can be made to support a person with a disability at work and are dependent on a situation. They may also be referred to as 'workplace accommodations'.

3.2   Reasonable adjustments are made to level the playing field between disabled and non-disabled employees. The purpose of this policy is to ensure the most effective adjustments are made and people are best supported with disabilities at work in a pro-active, collaborative manner.

3.3   Disabled people are not expected to know what reasonable adjustments will support them, but if they have an idea, these can be discussed collaboratively.

4 Requesting reasonable adjustments

4.1 A person disclosing a disability doesn't have to know what reasonable adjustments will support them, but if they have an idea, these can be discussed collaboratively.

4.2 To request reasonable adjustments, a person can email their line manager or alternative designated employee informing them that they have a disability impacting their work and would like adjustments to help them overcome this. This may be done at the same time as disclosing a disability.

4.3 As soon as reasonably possible, an initial conversation will be held between a person and their manager or other relevant employee to establish possible adjustments to overcome any specific challenges arising from the disability. If solutions are straightforward (e.g in terms of cost, sign-off, and time), they can be recorded, implemented, and notified to HR via email. A time should be set for a review of any adjustments made to ensure they are effective.

4.4 If the solution is not straightforward, such as requiring budget sign-off, or if solutions are unknown, the matter should be escalated to HR. If relevant, HR can coordinate the involvement of experts to help identify adjustments, such as making a referral to Occupational Health.

4.5 Unnecessary delays should be avoided, and interim measures should aim to be agreed upon and provided.

5 Independent Assessments

5.1 An independent assessment for the purposes of identifying adjustments involves a meeting between the disabled person and an independent third party with medical expertise to identify potential reasonable adjustments for that person at work. The purpose is to ensure the person is supported at work.

5.2 This may be to a standard Occupational Health professional, specialising in enabling an individual to undertake their occupation in a way that causes least harm to their health. Alternatively, or additionally, the independent assessment may be by a body with expertise in a particular condition, if necessary.

5.3 A referral and assessment may involve standard questions about the impact a disability may have on a person's ability to do their job, as this is important to understand to be able to provide the most effective support.

5.4 Following an assessment, a report should be provided to the employee and employer, and a follow-up discussion should be arranged with relevant employees, such as HR, the person's manager, and the person themselves.

6 Making reasonable adjustments

6.1 Following any external involvement, a conversation should take place with HR, the manager or otherwise designated employee and disabled person, to identify which reasonable adjustments will be made, how they will be implemented, and if the person is in employment, the dates for review. These adjustments should be recorded and stored in an accessible location for HR, the manager, and employee, or confirmed via email.

6.2 The adjustments to be made should be reasonable in relation to a specific set of circumstances. Factors to be considered when assessing the reasonableness of adjustments include its:

- effectiveness in reducing any disadvantages caused by a person's disability at work

- practicability, including of implementation, and potential alternatives

- implications on health and safety

- financial costs, including consideration of the availability of Access to Work, a Government scheme that can help fund adjustments, in relation to the size and resources of the company.

6.3 As much information and transparency should be provided to the disabled person as possible, at all times. This is important in terms of timeframes, interim support measures, the practical implementation of adjustments, and involvement of any other colleagues.

6.4 The dates and/or regularity of when the effectiveness of adjustments will be discussed should be agreed upon and scheduled in advance as a framework, though they can be discussed at any time. It is recognised that they may not necessarily be a 'fix' and needs may change over time.

6.5 In every situation, the aim is to ensure that the adjustments are effective and the disabled person is supported to do their job. However, if the adjustments are found to be ineffective and/or the person is unable to practically continue in their role, alternative support should be identified. Only as a measure of last resort, if no other options are available, the employee's contract may be terminated.

Chapter 2
Spotting ADHD at Work

Attention Deficit Hyperactivity Disorder is a **neurodevelopmental condition.** It's not an illness or a disease - it's just the way our brain works, and is something we have throughout our lives.

The diagnostic criteria requires symptoms of hyperactivity and/or impulsivity, and/or inattention to cause at least moderate 'pervasive' negative impairment in two or more 'important settings' of a person's life, including social, familial, educational, and/or occupational settings.[6]

Essentially, the symptoms have to 'disorder' our lives. The word 'disorder' is extremely unhelpful and stigmatising, especially as things definitely don't have to stay this way once we understand how our brain works, but this is why **not everybody has ADHD.**

---

6   https://www.nice.org.uk/guidance/ng87/resources/attention-deficit-hyperactivity-disorder-diagnosis-and-management-pdf-1837699732933

For example, we might all lose our keys from time to time, but we don't all get locked out of our house every month, repeatedly having to call the locksmith regardless of how many times it happens! Understanding I have ADHD has enabled me to stop beating myself up for things like this and accept my limitations instead, adapting my environment by giving trusted people copies of my keys!

As ADHD has only been diagnosable in UK adults since 2008, there's potentially millions of adults who have lived their entire life beating themselves up for having a disability that they didn't even know about. There's hundreds of thousands more on years long waiting lists for NHS assessments, waiting to access support for managing their ADHD.

In particular, women, girls and people of underrepresented racial backgrounds have been mis-diagnosed or left without support over the years, as the focus has been on young boys who disrupted the class. Girls like me, who were able to successfully hide the fact that they had no idea what was going on with invisible internal hyperactivity were left to disrupt only ourselves.

ADHD impacts every area of our life, because it's how we think, act, function, process and feel - it's basically the operating instructions for our brain. Work happens to be one of places where we spend the majority of our time as adults, and many workplaces have neuronormative expectations and standards where being neurodivergent may result in challenges requiring tailored support.

Finding out that you are neurodivergent can be extremely overwhelming, as you try to navigate what this means for you. To do so whilst working can be incredibly stressful, ranging from processing complicated emotions, to trying out new medication, and understanding whether it's something you should talk to your employer about - especially whilst it's something you're still processing yourself.

How can ADHD show up at work?

The 30% developmental delay in executive functioning skills related to ADHD means that we can find it very hard to 'do what we know', despite our best efforts. Ultimately, this 'delay' is in reference to the fact that our society upholds neuronormative standards, and these are simply differences. There are many positives associated with thinking differently, as set out in chapter 'ADHD Strengths'.

However, there are also many challenges that can arise as a result of being held to certain standards by society, and especially in work:

Self-awareness

People with ADHD may struggle to be aware of their feelings, needs, and experiences. Ways this could show up include sitting in uncomfortable positions and holding our breath without realising, forgetting to eat or take breaks, overworking, overcommitting, or generally speaking, living as a 'human doing' instead of a human being. We may also be prone to talking without realising that others aren't listening, or talk very fast, for example.

This can also result in challenges with understanding who 'we' are, making it difficult to know what we want from life - from our future goals, to how to spend the weekend. We may easily end up pleasing others and burning out, because we don't know how to prioritise ourselves. It's also why we may experience time as 'now' or 'not now', resulting in challenges with lateness and understanding what we might need in the future, such as packing or leaving the house!

Many people diagnosed with ADHD as adults will likely be unaware about what kind of support they need, particularly in the workplace - we just know we need help! This can make it very difficult to ask for help, and instead result in us suffering in silence until we burn out. We may also be very anxious about taking medication, in not understanding how this will impact our general day to day life with little reference point of what is 'normal'.

Having a difference in self-awareness to neurotypical people can be very difficult to manage, but it also leads us to live fully in the present, and can see us perform exceptionally well at work, in addition to supporting others. It's just important to have a healthy balance of this that isn't to our detriment, and to ensure that we access the same compassion we provide for others - including ourselves!

Building in support such as regular 1:1 meetings and breaks can be really helpful to support an employee with ADHD in becoming more self-aware, instead of acting on autopilot. It's important for us to build this skill to understand what kind of working environments we need in order to set ourselves up for success, especially in the long run!

Motivation

People with ADHD are said to have an 'interest based nervous system'.[7]

This means that if we're interested in something, we can hyper-focus and achieve an impossibly huge amount, but if we're not, this may simply just not happen.

Novelty, interest and adrenaline can make the first 80% of a task seem so much easier than the last 20%, because the dopamine rush of excitement has gone, requiring far more energy to 'follow through'. 'Easy' tasks like administration and self-care, and cleaning

7   https://www.additudemag.com/secrets-of-the-adhd-brain/

or cooking, can feel extremely challenging for an ADHD brain!

In the workplace, a common response to ADHD is to assume a person needs less work, but often we need *more* stimulating work that suits our interest based nervous system. Having support in place such as administrative help or task swapping between teams can make the world of difference, enabling us to harness our hyper-focus. This 'flow state' can see us achieve extraordinary things, and having a brain that thrives on challenge and stimulation is excellent for business!

This difference in motivation can make us very different to manage from neurotypical people, because we're not motivated in the same ways, as explained in chapter 'Managing ADHD for Success'. By understanding how to hack our own unique nervous system we can build this into our work as needed, applying our skills of hyper-focus to areas that are less interesting and stimulating.

In turn, this can also make us excellent managers, as we understand that everybody is motivated differently rather than assuming people will just do what they need to do. Personally, I'm constantly looking to understand how to best support the people I work with, and am extremely grateful to them in supporting me to finish off the things I can't do myself.

Emotional Regulation

People with ADHD may experience Rejection Sensitive Dysphoria, which is intense emotional pain associated with real or perceived rejection that lasts for a limited period of time. This isn't an official diagnosable condition, but is said to be exclusively linked with ADHD.[8]

Growing up beating yourself up for not being able to do the things you 'should' be able to do, or being 'normal', can understandably make us worried about doing life 'wrong'. This can result in communication challenges, social anxiety, and people pleasing, causing difficulties in relating to others - especially those who can help us through it.

At work, this can be particularly challenging, especially as work necessarily involves making mistakes and learning from them. We might hold ourselves to impossibly high standards, or overthink what we 'should' be doing - I used to experience intense anxiety over how to sign off an email, for example!

This can obviously cause challenges related to receiving and giving constructive feedback, as explained in chapter 'Resolving Workplace Challenges'. It's important that we strengthen the skills to distinguish between our thoughts, emotions

---

8   https://chadd.org/wp-content/uploads/2016/10/ATTN_10_16_EmotionalRegulation.pdf

and facts, so we don't chase the stories in our head of what we assume instead of what is actually happening. For example, I once ruminated over feedback that simply consisted of 'thanks', overthinking whether this wasn't good enough, or whether there was some hidden meaning behind it.

Giving an employee with ADHD positive feedback and encouragement is how to get the best out of them, empowering them with psychological safety and the knowledge that it's okay to make mistakes. There's no such thing as perfect, but having a working environment where expectations are clearly set out, broken down, and communicated, can make a huge difference in enabling us to know what we need to do to succeed.

Although these challenges in emotional regulation can be very challenging to experience, they also tend to make us extremely supportive, empathetic and caring towards others, because we know how tough rejection can feel! These are excellent qualities to have in employees, and can make us highly valued members of a team.

Problem Solving

Being neurodivergent means that we literally think differently to 'most' people, which by definition, makes us innovative problem solvers. I like to think of this as our ability to make 'creative adjustments' to living in a neurotypical world. This is a brilliant asset to any workplace, but can be challenging in contrast to the status quo of 'just how things are done'.

This isn't necessarily a bad thing, but these systems are there for a reason. People with ADHD often start at level 100 instead of level 1, and have to work backwards, using up considerable time and energy. We may have lots of brilliant ideas, but lack the energy or time to make them all happen. Or, as I often see, it's not actually our job!

Having a super fast brain can make it difficult for others - and ourselves - to keep up. We can also end up self sabotaging, experiencing procrastination, restlessness, perfectionism and burnout, whilst making things harder than they need to be.

I often work with people who steamroll into companies with lots of brilliant ideas, who immediately pick up on many inefficiencies, and have lots of excellent ideas to make things run better. Unfortunately, employers are not always so receptive to change, which can result in employees with ADHD feeling disengaged and embarrassed for sharing their vulnerability and passion at work.

This can be balanced in the workplace with opportunities to use our wonderfully creative and curious brains, and structures setting out instructions and processes in a clear and accessible way. It can also be very useful to have explanations of why things are the way they are, and regular opportunities for review. In my experience, people with ADHD have an incredible knack to spot improvements and innovations that everybody agrees is needed, so embrace the opportunity for change!

Impulsivity

People with ADHD may have a tendency to 'act before thinking'. This means we might be more prone to making reckless decisions, such as quitting our jobs, or saying things we'd later regret! We might also say yes to requests without thinking them through, and overcommit ourselves without realising.

This can make it hard to make and keep to decisions, as our brains are constantly seeking dopamine and distractions. Planning and organisation can become extremely complicated as a result, leaving us overwhelmed and burnt out as we undo the tangle of over-committing.

In the workplace, skills such as delegating and prioritising can be tough for people with ADHD because of our tendencies to do everything ourselves, or start new ideas without necessarily communicating these to others. For example, I once announced a podcast and invited speakers to talk on it, all before the person who would have to organise it had woken up to 100 emails about it!

Having frameworks and boundaries in place can help us to break down tasks and stick to strategies such as waiting before acting on our ideas. Realising that we don't have to do everything at once can free us to build up trust in ourselves, working towards 'sprints' instead of marathons - which tend to be much more ADHD friendly!

It's important to note that these impulsive qualities can be excellent assets in the workplace, as we trust our gut, and are inclined to take action where others might not. The secret is providing a container for us to do so in a structured way, allowing our lateral thinking to foster creativity and growth at work.

Memory

The memory challenges associated with ADHD can be very challenging to live with. I can have reminders plastered all over the walls of my flat, but still completely forget to do the thing I need to do. Forgetting appointments, conversations, decisions, and more can be extremely annoying - not only for myself, but those around me.

Ultimately, the way around this isn't to beat ourselves up, but to create systems that accommodate these challenges. We all live in a world of information overload, and it's impossible to remember everything, especially when we're living so fast.

Identifying what we need to remember by strengthening our ability to prioritise means we can create structures that do a lot of the work for us. The secret is making these simple, and accepting that they won't work forever - and that's okay.

Viewing these strategies as a test in understanding what works for our brain means we can take the pressure off and get creative, building on this with delegating and asking for help. Having extra 1:1s and reminders from other people at work can be extremely useful. One simple example is that when I work in a co-working space, I remember to eat lunch because I see people around me eating!

Ironically, knowing that I have these memory challenges tends to make me quite organised from the outset, as I operate in a mode of knowing I need to do something 'now' or I might forget it. They also mean people with ADHD may forget failure and mistakes very quickly, learning the lessons they need to bounce back up and try again, making us extremely resilient!

Understanding how these executive functioning differences can show up at work is often the secret of managing our ADHD, instead of being managed by it.

ADHD & Executive Functioning Skills Quiz

This quiz can help someone understand how ADHD impacts them, by rating their challenges in the below areas.

QUESTIONS	RATING SCALE				
	Never	Rarely	Sometimes	Often	Always
Self-awareness e.g being unaware of feelings, needs or experiences, burnout	○	○	○	○	○
Problem solving e.g difficulty breaking tasks down, decision paralysis	○	○	○	○	○
Inhibition (impulsivity) e.g 'acting before thinking', challenges finishing tasks	○	○	○	○	○
Motivation e.g 'interest-based nervous system' - hyperfocus vs procrastination	○	○	○	○	○
Emotional Regulation e.g experiencing intense emotions, Rejection Sensitive Dysphoria	○	○	○	○	○
Memory e.g forgetting appointments, information & instructions	○	○	○	○	○

Chapter 3
Disclosing ADHD at work

For the purposes of this book, 'disclosure' is when a person tells their potential or current employer about the fact they have (or may have) ADHD. When the employer becomes aware of an actual or potential disability, legal duties are triggered for them under the Equality Act 2010. This being said, a person may not necessarily realise they are disclosing a disability to their employer by telling them about ADHD, or intend to do so.

Regardless, an employer should be aware of this, and either way, an employee (or employer) not being aware that a disclosure of disability has taken place does not impact the duties triggered under the Equality Act.

Disclosure can be very difficult to do - and even the word 'disclosure' can feel intimidating, as though we are sharing information that was previously hidden. As an employee, you are under no obligation to tell your employer about any health conditions or disabilities, but it's much harder for them to support you with a working environment tailored to your specific needs if they don't know!

In an ideal world, talking about ADHD at work should be a positive thing, because you're sharing part of who you are with your workplace, and trusting them to accept and support you as you are. In return, employers can foster diverse and inclusive work-places, with a foundation of psychological safety.

However, the route to disclose ADHD to an em-ployer can feel very vulnerable. There's also not usually an obvious reason or method of doing so, so to bring it up in conversation might feel very awkward and formal. We might also assume our employers know if we share something on social media about having ADHD, for example, but this might leave them in a legally grey area.

It can also feel unclear about who an 'employer' amounts to - whether this is our colleagues, manag-ers, HR, or somebody else. This will depend on the situation, but hopefully anybody in a line manage-ment position would have had sufficient training to know what to do next.

This can all be made a million times easier by employ-ers providing a publicly accessible neurodiversity policy explaining how someone can disclose a condition like ADHD at work. This could explain concepts like 'disa-bility', 'reasonable adjustments' and 'disclosure', the next steps involved, and provide resources to make this easier, such as email templates to use.

Why disclose ADHD at work?

There are a huge range of reasons why someone may wish to disclose ADHD at work, ranging from simply wanting to share this with their team, to seeking out support.

Here are some of the scenarios where disclosure may be relevant:

1) Application stage

The Equality Act covers potential workers, meaning employers must ensure that recruitment processes are accessible to all. Examples of why a person may wish to disclose ADHD when applying for a job may include a need for adjustments during the interview process, or in reference to their work experience or CV. They also may simply wish to be open about this from the start, to understand how neurodiversity-friendly their potential employer may be, and see this as an important part of who they are.

Many organisations guarantee an interview for disabled people who meet the minimum criteria of a job role, which can be helpful. Even so, when I've done this, it has felt a bit like a checkbox (literally!), and someone needs to understand they have a disability in the first place to disclose this.

It's easiest for employers to share any neurodiversity policies alongside job adverts, which should hopefully explain concepts such as disability and provide reassurance about disclosure at this stage. It's important to remember that you don't have to if you don't want to - an employer has no right to know, and disclosure should only be for your benefit.

2) Interview stage

If you have disclosed ADHD during an application stage, you will often be asked, 'do you require any adjustments at interview?'. This is a vague and difficult question to answer, especially for someone who isn't sure what they need, or what a potential interview process will involve.

It's also a risk, as there's no guarantee of these adjustments being granted, which can create a highly stressful environment for neurodivergent people who may already struggle with interviews. For example, people I know have been refused access to the interview questions in advance with no reasons provided. This is frustrating, because this could likely be viewed as a failure to make reasonable adjustments by the Employment Tribunal, but it's unlikely that the person would have the resources to complain about this.

Instead, the employer would have lost brilliant potential employees as a result of their inaccessibility.

The benefit for the individual is being able to avoid wasting their time with applying for jobs at organisations that are unlikely to accommodate them in the long term, but this can obviously be very upsetting to experience.

In contrast, I've seen other employers go the extra mile when someone has disclosed ADHD at an interview stage, such as by offering a phone call to chat through what the process would look like, and explore any changes that could be made to accommodate them.

Adjustments such as providing questions or tasks in advance, allowing written notes or fidget toys to be taken in, having interviews remotely, allowing a person to view the environment beforehand, removing psychometric tests, or simply having a chat about the process can make a huge difference to neurodivergent people in interviews but this will be ultimately be dependent on the individual. Even so, providing examples of adjustments that have been implemented for others can be very helpful. This ultimately helps employers to find the best person for the job, by ensuring everybody is able to access the same opportunities to perform at interview.

3) Onboarding stage

The most common answer I've had when talking to employers about their disability policy is that they 'ask about it when onboarding a new employee.' This usually looks like asking someone 'do you have a disability?' Firstly, this isn't a disability policy! A policy should be written down, repeatable, relevant, and as accessible as possible, especially by those it's about.

Secondly, telling your new employer on your first day that you have ADHD and that you believe this amounts to a disability can feel very intimidating, especially given the stigma and shame surrounding this language. This is assuming you even understand that ADHD can be a disability, which many people wouldn't, as it's not exactly something we're told when being diagnosed, and is highly situational.

This is especially anxiety inducing if there is no guarantee of what happens next, such as an accessible policy about disability or neurodiversity explaining processes such as Occupational Health assessments. It may be more effective for employers to provide links to these policies alongside any questions relating to them, in addition to providing time for an individual to read, process, understand, and discuss their options properly.

It would be ideal for employers to know that an employee is neurodivergent as soon as practically possible, to ensure they are supported at work from the outset. Being aware that an employee with ADHD is starting, for example, may enable employers to ensure appropriate neurodiversity training, such as for their manager, has taken place before they start.

4) Probation stage

Probation can be highly stressful for everybody, but in my experience, especially so for neurodivergent people. This artificial time period where you could be fired at any time can result in increased stress, which ironically results in increased challenges relating to executive functioning, such as emotional regulation and organisation.

I've heard from many people how they plan to disclose ADHD to their employer after they pass probation. This means putting themselves through needless stress out of fear that they'll be fired if they ask for help, ironically resulting in increased challenges with ADHD impacting performance. It's much better to feel safe in disclosure straight away to be supported to create the working environment where you can thrive long term.

Employers can provide this with policies as explained above, and clearly explaining that disclosure does not impact probation or employment opportunities at all. As an individual, you should never be treated negatively as a result of disclosure, and disclosing during your probation should actually provide you with additional, not less, legal protection and stability at work.

It can also feel much harder to disclose this after your probation period ends, especially in ruminating on whether you'll be in trouble for not disclosing this earlier on or whether the fact you didn't proves that you don't need adjustments to do your job - even if you've suffered in silence! Despite these very valid concerns, the law is the law: you are deserving of support at any time that you need it, regardless of what's led up to that point.

Hopefully employers can provide reassurance in policies and communications around the fact that disclosure is welcomed at any time, which would go a long way in boosting psychological safety at work!

It's likely that at this point onwards an individual may let their manager know instead of, or in addition to HR, as they're less likely to have day to day communications with HR. This means that managers should have support and appropriate training to ensure they feel confident knowing what to do in case of disclosure and how to provide effective support. Again, this can be very simply set out in an accessible disability, neurodiversity, and/or reasonable adjustments policy.

As an individual disclosing, it's important to remember that your manager may not know how to respond straight away, but that they ultimately want to support you to do your job in the best way for you. Managers have a lot of expectations on them to have all of the answers, so any fear they have about saying the wrong thing may be miscommunicated. If you're not happy with your manager's response to your ADHD, it's advisable to get another opinion, such as from HR.

Managers who haven't been trained may feel anxious and prefer to leave conversations about ADHD and adjustments to HR, which may result in tensions and misunderstandings. HR professionals themselves may also feel scared about saying the wrong thing, so it's important to be compassionate, vulnerable, and clear within these conversations. They can be scary for everybody, but they don't have to be!

Ideally, these conversations would simply be 'human to human', enabling everybody to feel psychologically safe and confident, understanding that nobody is expected to have all of the answers, and everybody is doing their best. Giving a person the tools to pass their probation period seems like common sense, setting them up for future success in their role.

5) When applying for Access to Work
Access to Work (ATW) is a UK Government grant that can help fund support to help people with health conditions to stay in work. The scheme applies for

people who live and work (or are about to start or return to work) in England, Scotland or Wales - there's a different system in Northern Ireland.[9]

Awards could cover things like ADHD coaching, administrative support, software, equipment, support with travel, awareness training, and more. At the time of writing, up to £66,000 is available per person, per year. It's one of the best kept secrets of the Government, as a very small number of people know about it!

A person can apply for ATW online or by phone. If they're employed, they'll have to put the contact details of their 'employer' to confirm their employment status. In my experience, this is when many people in the UK will inform their employer about their ADHD.

It's important that employers familiarise themselves with these processes and support people to apply where needed. For example, it may be unclear whether someone is intending to disclose ADHD for

---

9 Like everything in this book, this information is correct at the time of writing based off my experiences and understanding. However, Access to Work can be extremely complicated to understand, and change quickly, so always check the Government website for the most up to date information.

A factsheet for employers is available here: https://www.gov.uk/government/publications/access-to-work-guide-for-employers/access-to-work-factsheet-for-employers

A factsheet for applicants is available here: https://www.gov.uk/government/publications/access-to-work-factsheet/access-to-work-factsheet-for-customers

the purpose of a disability in terms of seeking adjustments, or whether they are simply intending to notify their employer about applying for ATW.

It may also be difficult for an individual to know whose details to put down, which can be complicated further if an employer is unaware of ATW. All that's needed is for someone to confirm that an individual works at that organisation, like a reference for a rental contract. At the time of writing, applications take 6 months to process, so this is a long grey area with the potential for a lot of confusion, as set out in chapter 'Navigating Access to Work'. In an ideal world, the process would be set out in a clearly accessible policy.

6) During employment

An individual may wish to disclose ADHD at work at any time during their employment. There's a huge range of reasons for this, but naturally, one may be that they have learned that they may or do have ADHD (or someone they care for does, such as a child) and would like to understand what support is available to them at work.

Having collaborative, curious, and compassionate conversations, hopefully rooted in an accessible policy explaining relevant options, steps, and timelines, can result in people accessing the support they need to reduce or remove any challenges they may be experiencing at work because of ADHD.

If you're an individual wondering whether to talk to your employer about this, I'd recommend looking at whether they have any policies or resources on neurodiversity, disability, health conditions or adjustments. If not, try talking to someone you trust about your options. It can be helpful to think about what kinds of outcomes you'd like from such conversations, even if it's simply to understand what support is available in case you need it.

It also may feel easier to write this down in an email, especially if you'd like some kind of specific support from your employer - everybody is different and this will depend on your situation at work. Asking for specific timelines and communication can be helpful, including any adjustments about how you want this process to go, such as by having it all via email.

Ultimately, disclosing ADHD at work should lead to positive outcomes for everybody, as a person will hopefully be supported to create the best working environment for them to thrive within. However, if cultures are not in place where people feel safe to do so, this can feel very anxiety inducing.

7) When there's a problem

If workplaces are not set up with inclusive and supportive cultures enabling people to be open about having ADHD from the start of their employment, they may become aware of this only when problems arise, such as in relation to performance or absences.

This kind of disclosure can be very difficult to navigate. My personal opinion about ADHD is that it can explain certain behaviours, but not excuse them. It's our responsibility to do what we can to understand how our brain works and access the support we need, and our employer's responsibility to provide a safe and supportive environment for us to do that within. When this doesn't happen, there may be a breakdown in communications resulting in conflict, as in chapter 'Resolving Workplace Challenges'.

8) Stress or a change in personal circumstances

ADHD symptoms may worsen with stress, and particularly when our environments change. For example, I see this happen a lot with menopause, new parents, bereavement, people who have new jobs and people who have new managers. When our environments change quite suddenly, it can take us a while to understand how to re-centre ourselves.

It's important that ADHD is considered in this context to ensure that a person is accessing the support they need at all times. Although everyone experiences stressful situations, the difference for people with ADHD is that this can have a significant impact on our performance due to the differences we experience in executive functioning. This is why everything might start to feel like it's falling apart in all areas of our life if we experience something like an argument with a loved one.

The best solution is to take a break and be kind to yourself, and having an employer who can understand and support you with this is key to avoiding burnout.

Should ADHD be disclosed at work?

If you have ADHD, it's important to remember that the decision to tell your employer is ultimately your choice, and you should consider all of the factors available to you. Although it would be great if employers had clear processes set out that everybody followed, in reality, what happens next is highly dependent on the individuals involved and is very difficult to predict. The law offers protection from negative treatment, but unfortunately, this doesn't necessarily guarantee that it won't happen.

You deserve to be treated with respect and support at work, and I hope you have an environment where you feel safe enough to ask for the help you need. If you are feeling nervous about this, you may wish to find someone at your work to talk to informally about this to better understand your options, such as if you have an ADHD Champion in your workplace, any neurodiversity employee networks or general wellbeing / mental health champions or leads.

There are great benefits to disclosing ADHD at work, such as the ability to simply be yourself in the workplace and access the support you may need, but stigma does exist and it can feel very stressful to navigate this, especially if you're not sure what should happen next. My best advice is to talk to someone you trust, take your time, and be kind to yourself. It doesn't change who you are!

Template: Disclosing ADHD at work

If you'd like to disclose your ADHD to your employer, you may wish to use this email template, adding in the relevant purpose as needed. Using the formal language of disability and disclosure makes it clear that you consider your ADHD to be a disability requiring support as legally required. However, you may not see your ADHD as a disability and simply wish to let them know - so feel free to edit it as feels appropriate for you.

Subject line: Disclosure of Disability

Dear (name),

I wanted to let you know that I have Attention Deficit Hyperactivity Disorder, which has a long term, substantial and negative effect on my ability to do normal activities as my colleagues are able to.

This being said, research links many strengths such as divergent thinking, the ability to hyper-focus, and resilience with ADHD.[10]

I am still learning about the condition and how it affects me, but I hope that disclosing this disability to you will lead to an effective working environment where these strengths can be harnessed, and challenges can be supported.

---

10   https://link.springer.com/article/10.1007/s12402-018-0277-6

In terms of next steps, I would appreciate:

- Being signposted to and understanding any standard company processes and next steps in relation to disclosing a disability, such as any relevant policies.

- Reassurance of how this discussion can be picked up when I feel clearer about what I would like to happen next.

- Understanding any support that may be available and how I can access this e.g via the UK Government's Access to Work fund supporting people with health conditions at work.

Thank you very much in advance for your help with this.

Kind wishes,
[Name]

Supporting ADHD

Chapter 4
Creating an ADHD friendly culture

Train for inclusivity

I am often asked by employers about how they can make their cultures inclusive and accessible for neurodivergent people. This is ironic, given how impossible I found it to get a job!

It's hard to help someone if you don't know what kinds of struggles they're experiencing. This also goes for the person - I had no idea that I had ADHD until turning 25, after years of ruminating over job applications, impulsively quitting any kind of employment I managed to get after accepting it, and beating myself up before starting over again in a new industry!

The first step is education: gaining an understanding of what neurodiversity actually means, and how this can contribute to a workplace. Having mandatory training for employees, especially HR and managers, on neurodiversity, disability, and inclusivity is extremely important to ensure that everybody takes responsibility for inclusivity. It can also be very helpful for people who may be unaware that they are neurodivergent - I learned much more about my ADHD from a 'lunch and learn' session at work than from my psychiatrist!

Discrimination is often a result of ignorance, and a fear of vulnerability. People are afraid to get things wrong, and to offend others, which is what creates cultures where important conversations go unspoken. By having open conversations and transparency within an organisation, and providing shame-free spaces where people can ask questions without any fear of judgement, organisations can unite as a collective with understanding and empathy.

This training can be done remotely or in person, such as the sessions I provide. Having training from a person with lived experience is important to literally bring this to life, and it tends to be much more engaging for everybody. It's also very difficult to offend me (try being a fashion model!). During these sessions, I always try to remind everyone that there are no right or wrong answers, and zero expectation on anybody to be experts. Language and the meaning of concepts like neurodiversity are constantly in flux - ADHD wasn't even diagnosable in adults until 2008 in the UK!

It may understandably feel overwhelming to access this training as an employer, especially when the topic is so sensitive. Whilst corporate umbrella training on neurodiversity may seem to cover all areas, it's important not to treat education as a box ticking exercise. The reason ADHD Works' training (and this book!) focuses mainly on ADHD, is because it's impossible to cover all neurodevelopmental conditions in an authentic and high quality way.

Holding general training on neurodiversity awareness can be helpful, but it's important that this is of high quality and is attended by everybody who needs to attend. Otherwise, the people who may be in most need of this education (such as people who may hold incorrect beliefs about neurodiversity, for example), may not attend or benefit from the training.

It's also impossible to be fully prepared for every kind of potential neurodivergent condition that may arise, especially as this may manifest differently in everybody. If employers have clear policies and processes in place, they can consider in depth training on a case by case basis as soon as they become aware of a need to do so at work, such as somebody disclosing ADHD.

In these situations, I strongly believe that accessing condition-specific training for an individual's manager, and possibly their team, should be a priority. As in chapter, 'Managing ADHD for Success', managing a neurodivergent person is very different to managing a neurotypical person, and may contradict previous management training techniques. As an employee will have the most day to day inter-action with their manager and team, it's important that colleagues understand how to provide the most effective support.

Generally speaking, employers should consider whether there are ways of working or physical features that could cause a 'substantial disadvan-tage' to disabled employees or applicants in general - and address these without waiting for someone to ask for help! This is why having strong and open communication lines with well-supported Employee Resource Groups and networks is important within the workplace. This is especially important to do whenever there's a significant change to the way things are done, such as everybody working from home during the Covid-19 pandemic!

Share best practice

Organisations that gain this understanding and truly value neurodiversity and the strengths it brings should shout about it! I don't believe in trying to 'sell' someone on the values of inclusivity, because it's obvious. Our society is made up of people from all different walks of life - 1 in 7 people are neurodiver-gent.[11]

---

11 https://www.local.gov.uk/lga-libdem-group/our-press-releases/
neurodiversity#:~:text=Most%20people%20are%20neurotypical%2C%20
meaning,learns%20and%20processes%20information%20differently.

As an organisation, it makes sense to have this representation within your organisation. For example, it's ironic that only 5% of solicitors have disclosed a disability vs 14% of the working population, because trust is such a core pillar of seeking legal advice.[12]

If I know a lawyer thinks like me, and has ADHD, I would be far more likely to go to them than a neurotypical lawyer! I'd guess this would be similar for most industries, because we naturally gravitate towards people like us.

On a practical level, this looks like publicly valuing neurodiversity, such as by sharing blog posts, or podcasts with neurodivergent employees. For example, we have a brilliant podcast episode featuring a manager and the person she managed, who disclosed that she was on a waiting list for an ADHD assessment, before later receiving a diagnosis.

The manager explained how sharing her own experiences in anxiety and doing her own research about ADHD helped them to work together in a compassionate and collaborative way, despite not having all of the answers. It really is as simple as treating others how you'd like to be treated, and having employees in senior leadership positions seek the support they need empowers others to do the same. Providing opportunities for employees to

12   https://www.sra.org.uk/sra/equality-diversity/diversity-profession/diverse-legal-profession/

share their experiences as they would like, both internally and externally, is a great way of demonstrating best practice to others, along with organisational commitment to neurodivergent people.

I would be much more likely to apply for a job if I knew someone else at an organisation had ADHD as well! Sharing real life experiences from individuals who feel comfortable with this is much more effective than signing up to pledges or schemes, and helps everybody. Initiatives such as training and events can help this to happen naturally, such as enabling people to connect over a common interest in neurodiversity by attending the same event.

It's especially helpful for senior employees and leaders to share their experiences with neurodiversity, actively demonstrating that disclosing a disability does not prevent an employee from career progression. We can't be what we can't see!

Being open about our experiences can also help everybody else to improve their working practices. For example, I once knew a highly successful CEO who changed his working practices with his administrative assistants, changing it from the complicated and bureaucratic structure established by a consultancy company to one that worked for his brain. He explained that this was because he had ADHD, which resulted in many other people working in the organisation disclosing their own ADHD or other neurodivergent conditions, and how they had also been struggling with this structure. Sharing our experiences empowers others to do the same.

Sharing best practice also applies for policies on things like reasonable adjustments and neurodiversity. For example, I made the reasonable adjustments template in chapter 'Disability vs Diversity' publicly available for anybody to use, and was delighted to see a company adapt and implement this within their organisation. They published it on their website and shared how beneficial it had been to do for everybody in a public blog post. This was completely free, easy, and sets clear expectations and trust for current and potential employees - both neurodivergent and not.

Inclusivity benefits everybody - not just the individual it's about. Practically speaking, reasonable adjustments don't necessarily need to only apply to something like ADHD or a disability. There are all kinds of reasons why someone may need support from work, such as bereavement or family members experiencing challenges needing extra help, and having the mechanisms in place for anybody to access support helps foster psychological safety throughout the organisation. Helping people empowers everybody to work in the ways that work best for them.

At a talk I did, the host said 'You can ask questions in the chat, anonymously, or unmute yourself to ask directly', which was a wonderfully simple example of inclusivity that benefits everybody, as it's accommodating a range of options. It doesn't have to be complicated! This also goes for office environments, such as by having quieter areas for people to concentrate in silence where needed. Going beyond labels to look at challenges and providing a range of solutions to support everybody, shockingly, does actually help everybody.

Many organisations have neurodiversity initiatives, where they actively seek to hire neurodivergent people. There can be certain areas where organisations may wish to hire people who think in a certain way and focus on these skills - I met a Director of one of the world's biggest technology companies by chance who told me their best employees were neurodivergent!

From my own experience, there are endless highly talented people with ADHD looking for work at ADHD Works in the search of an organisation that openly and actively welcomes neurodivergent people.

A public commitment to supporting neurodiversity doesn't have to include signing up to a scheme - it can be as simple as sharing examples of reasonable adjustments that have been made for other neurodivergent people on an intranet. Although everybody will be different, sharing some examples can help to provide a reference for people who may feel overwhelmed and unsure of where to start.

Providing public reassurance about 'untraditional career backgrounds' can also be helpful at an interview or recruitment stage, as many people with ADHD may have had squiggly careers. I've worked with people who have incredibly impressive careers in a range of different areas throughout their lives, from working as a chef to qualifying as an electrician, and starting their own businesses to going back to university to begin a new degree, but who have felt a lot of shame in applying for jobs because of this. This includes myself - I was extremely embarrassed of changing my mind so much in my career, and felt like I had to reshape my CV for any job I applied for.

Celebrating our differences and keeping an open mind about the learnings and strengths a person picks up through an unusual path will mean they're more likely to share them at work - which is in everybody's interest!

Awareness vs action

In my experience, there's a lot of 'awareness' building around neurodiversity in organisations, but much less action. It's easy to talk about being inclusive, but much harder to actually foster cultures that support people to be themselves at work.

This is why I created an 'ADHD Champions' programme for an organisation whose medical insurer was starting to cover neurodiversity assessments.

As this meant they'd be more likely to have lots of people suddenly navigating neurodiversity at work, they were able to train their employees to support each other in creating working environments where they could thrive.

Instead of simply sharing knowledge, such as by explaining what ADHD is and how it shows up, employees left with the skills and abilities of understanding how to put this into practice. This is the difference between a workplace that pays lip service to inclusivity with check boxes, and one that truly embraces it and harnesses the benefits it brings.

Having an inclusive and supportive workplace where everybody can thrive as themselves makes for a happy organisation. I've seen organisations who've been scared of supporting an employee with ADHD because 'then everybody else would want the same'.

Presumably not everybody else would need the same support (even those with ADHD, as we're all unique), but even if they did - what's wrong with this, if they need it? As in 'Disability vs Diversity', making reasonable adjustments to accommodate disabled people at work isn't a choice - it's a legal requirement - but the purpose of this is to level up the playing field.

Unequal treatment may be required in order to achieve equality, including treating a disabled worker more 'favourably' than others. Protection from disability discrimination is not symmetrical, and so reverse claims of disability discrimination are not possible.

This law and formality should hopefully be a last resort for employers who cultivate inclusive and diverse workplace cultures. In an ideal world, employers would want people who are working at their organisation to be as happy and productive as possible. This means working in environments where they can thrive as they are, as opposed to ones where people are held back from being themselves.

The secret to this is equipping people with the skills to build trust with one another. There's no point in having a reasonable adjustments policy if nobody follows it. Too often, I see people go through Occupational Health processes after disclosing ADHD at work which are never discussed again, and the recommendations for adjustments are not implemented. The best efforts in the world at inclusivity mean nothing if it's just lip service. Hiring neurodivergent employees means you have a responsibility to support them with working environments where they can flourish and thrive, not simply tick a box. This benefits nobody!

These skills look like knowledge, in having training on the fundamentals of neurodiversity, in addition to ensuring the relevant people understand how to signpost employees towards relevant resources and support. Training people in listening and coaching skills can empower them to feel confident navigating any conversation, because they know they don't need to have the answers or a solution - they can help people to identify what this is for themselves.

Having ADHD specific coaching training can be particularly useful. Being able to help a person establish the purpose of a conversation and ground them within this, helping them to stay on track and avoid tangents, whilst providing a safe, judgement-free space, can see amazing results - whether they have ADHD or not! These skills are set out in further detail in chapter 'ADHD Coaching Skills'.

ADHD isn't (just) a 'HR thing'

It's normal for managers to not know how to respond to a disclosure of ADHD at work, and to see this as a 'HR matter'. I've worked with many managers who have had limited management training overall, having been promoted into their earlier role for being good at their job - let alone any specific training on supporting employees with disabilities at work.

Unless a clear policy and structure is in place for managers around reasonable adjustments, it's most likely that they will seek advice on what to do next from HR. As a result, this conversation can often end up drifting off into the atmosphere, with no clear timeframes or next steps set out as responsibility is delegated to HR.

This can cause extreme anxiety for a person with ADHD, who may be able to think about nothing else other than their potential impending doom, as their manager continues to assign them work as though nothing has changed.

If a person has told their manager about ADHD, please know how excruciating this is likely to be for them - especially if they are not given a clear response. It can easily send us into fight or flight mode, making it very difficult to relax and act as though nothing has changed in the interim.

When conversations about ADHD drift off into things the individual has to chase themselves, this can feel extremely humiliating and difficult to do. Providing as much reassurance, time frames, information and clarity as possible is never a bad thing.

Even if HR formally records disclosure or supports with managing processes around adjustments, this is fundamental to the relationship between the manager and the person they manage. It isn't possible to separate something like ADHD into a neat box: it's literally how we think, and will be relevant at all times.

Obviously, no medical information such as a person having ADHD should be shared with others on their behalf unless strictly necessary and with their permission, but an individual may like certain colleagues to be aware or receive training around ADHD, for example.

Finding the balance can be tricky. I've worked with mangers who have had a very tough time in understanding how to set boundaries around ADHD, such as in relation to conversations employees have initiated around medication. Ultimately, this will depend on the situation, but ensuring managers feel confident and supported is key to ensuring that collaborative and compassionate conversations happen for the benefit of everybody.

As in chapter 'Spotting ADHD at Work', people with ADHD may experience challenges with self-awareness and communication, so being clear on expectations and responsibilities is very important. Having these written down, for example in an 'ADHD Action Plan', can be extremely effective in fostering inclusive and accessible cultures for people with ADHD at work.

ADHD Action Plan

This sets out how a person feels about navigating their ADHD at work, and the roles of the people who are involved in supporting them, such as their manager or any relevant HR colleagues.

An ADHD Action Plan also sets out the specific challenges an individual may experience because of their ADHD at work, alongside expectations required of them within the workplace, such as certain deliverables and projects. Having the adjustments and strategies to support them written down in one place can be extremely helpful in knowing what has definitely been agreed.

For example, this could include the ability to work from home when a person with ADHD feels stressed without having to sign this off as sick leave, or having instructions given to them in a certain way. This means that everybody has a touch point and reminder in case things change, such as a new project with a new team or manager.

Importantly, this plan also sets out their strengths, as it's important to note that ADHD is simply differences in thinking: not deficits. Highlighting strengths alongside challenges is a great strategy to easily and regularly boost a person's self-esteem. Finally, any other important information can be recorded, such as Access to Work applications, medical appointments, and medication, if this feels relevant to share. For me it's something I would appreciate sharing, because then I know I've set this out in case there are any changes, such as if I forget to take it one day!

Ultimately, having a document like this can support

HR, managers, teams and individuals to understand how to work together in the most collaborative and effective way. ADHD doesn't have to be spoken about every day, but having additional context of how a person works best in light of thinking in this way and the support that's in place to help them to thrive is extremely important to maintain inclusive and supportive cultures in the long run.

Although an ADHD Action Plan is specific to ADHD, there are many different kinds available that may be helpful for everybody on a team to have and share with each other to provide ongoing support. For example, the charity Mind has excellent Wellness Action Plans, which are relevant to everybody, as we all 'have' mental health![13]

---

13 https://www.mind.org.uk/media/12145/mind-wellness-action-plan-workplace.pdf

Template:
ADHD Action Plan

These template ADHD Action Plans can be adapted as needed to support an individual with ADHD at work. If you have ADHD, remember that you don't necessarily need to share this with anybody, and can adapt it as needed - it can be very useful for us to have as a visual reminder of the ways in which we work best.

ADHD
Action Plan

What is expected of you at work?
e.g your working hours,
locations, expectations

What helps you work effectively?
e.g written instructions, 1:1s,
lunch breaks, medication

What are your challenges?
e.g time management,
focus, communication

What are your unique strengths?
e.g from the VIA Character
Strengths survey

ADHD
Action Plan

Are there signs you may be struggling?
e.g avoiding tasks, conflict, talking on too much

If so, what support would be helpful?
e.g someone asking if you're okay, or contacting someone else

What strategies can you put in place?
e.g exercise, taking breaks, therapy daily objectives

Anything else to note?
e.g medical appointments, medication colleagues to speak to about ADHD, Access to Work applications

Chapter 5
Reasonable Adjustments for ADHD

As in 'Disability vs Diversity' the Equality Act 2010 requires an employer to take reasonable steps to remove, reduce, or prevent the substantial disadvantage that a disabled person (including employees and job applicants) experiences at work because of their condition. This could include changes to physical features, the way things are done, or providing an auxiliary aid or service.

Although there's guidance[14] available to accompany this law, it can be very difficult to actually understand what this practically looks like in practice on an individual basis, as it will be different for everyone! This is especially so when it comes to an invisible condition like ADHD.

---

14   https://www.equalityhumanrights.com/en/multipage-guide/ employing-people-workplace-adjustments

https://www.equalityhumanrights.com/en/multipage-guide/ employment-workplace-adjustments

https://www.equalityhumanrights.com/en/publication-download/ employment-statutory-code-practice

The legalities involved can also make talking about reasonable adjustments feel formal and intimidating, but they don't have to be. There can also be a tendency to assume adjustments will cost money, but many are completely free - the average cost of an adjustment is £75.[15] These can also be referred to as 'workplace accommodations'.

Ultimately, reasonable adjustments are aimed at helping people to work in the best environments for them, that support their needs and enable them to do their job effectively. In a supportive, inclusive workplace, the majority of adjustments should be able to be made quickly and simply, welcomed as a part of enabling a person to work in the ways that suit them. If we imagine a house plant that isn't doing too well, we wouldn't immediately throw it out. We'd change its environment, maybe trying out more or less water, soil, or moving it closer to a window, for example.

This is a collaborative process: the plant can't talk explicitly to us to tell us what it needs, but we can figure it out together. For a person who is unsure what support they need, but they just know they might need something, the process is quite similar: it should be approached with collaboration, compassion, and creativity.

---

15   https://www.peoplebusiness.co.uk/disability-advice-for-employers/

Supporting a person to adapt their working environment to suit their unique brain wiring is an ongoing process, but equipping them with the tools and safety to do so in an independent and trusted way creates a foundation of psychological safety.

It doesn't have to be so formal as emailing to request a specific reasonable adjustment, or have to feel like you're being 'difficult' somehow - with the right culture in place, this can be viewed as a positive. As a business owner myself, I always celebrate the people we work with when they tell me the best working environments for them or ask for help. Developing our self-awareness and ability to access the support we need helps us to do the best job we can at work - sustainably!

Reasonable adjustments are a collaborative effort. Once we understand we have ADHD for example, it becomes our responsibility to do something about it. ADHD can explain things, but it doesn't excuse them. Implementing strategies and learnings for ourselves to understand our challenges and ask for the support we need where we can't do anymore underpins the 'reasonable' element of these adjustments.

For example, you may struggle with distractions in the office, so wish to work from a quiet area of the office. This is the contrast between independent-ly going by yourself to a quiet area to work from (if available!), versus asking for your own personal sound-proof office. On the flip slide, sometimes we might need the flexibility of working from home, if we are overstimulated by even the smallest noises, so having the freedom to do this when needed can be a huge help. Everybody will be different, but as a neurodivergent person, the responsibility starts with us in taking responsibility for ourselves.

An employer gets involved when they need to be. For example, if you are contractually obliged to work from the office, then your employer (presumably HR, who are responsible for setting policies, practices, and procedures within an organisation), may need to actively consent to you not doing so.

What is reasonable?

Employers only have a duty to implement adjustments if they are 'reasonable', so a balance must be made regarding reasonable adjustments.

For example, I chose to live in a flat over the road from my employer because I would get so anxious on public transport during busy periods that I'd often have panic attacks because of my ADHD, including stressing about lateness and sensory overwhelm. In this scenario it would be unreasonable for the average person in my position to have been expected to have lived over the road from their office (especially if you already had a place to live, which I didn't!), but an employer might be able to help with adjustments focused on these specific challenges.

An easy adjustment could have been to allow working from home or working with flexible hours, which my employer had in place for everybody anyway. This would have meant I could have avoided rush hour travel and the disadvantages that I experienced because of my ADHD. An unreasonable expectation on them would have maybe been requiring them to pay for my rent over the road, as there were alternatives such as this available!

Only a tribunal can determine what is 'reasonable'. However, there's a range of factors that can be considered in determining the reasonableness of an adjustment. These include:

- The size of an organisation: a large one is likely to be required to do more than a smaller one, given their wider access to resources and insurance.

- The size of a team: this may be relevant for the ease of redistributing work as needed, for example.

- The effectiveness of the adjustment in removing or reducing the disadvantage: expert opinions can be helpful here, such as recommendations from Occupational Health.

- The practicalness of the adjustment: as in, how easy and realistic is it to implement? Would any disruption be caused to the business or colleagues, and if so, how much?

- The financial or other costs of making the adjustment, and the extent of the financial and other resources of the organisation

- The availability of alternative support, including financial, to make the adjustment: this is where Access to Work may become confusing, as in chapter 'Navigating Access to Work'. They may be able to help pay for support, especially if an organisation can't afford it, but typically will provide help above and beyond a reasonable adjustment.

- The type and size of employer

- Any health and safety implications of the adjustment.

- Whether the adjustment would put those with another protected characteristic, who would be afforded protection by the Equality Act also, at a disadvantage as a result.

Ultimately, what is reasonable will be dependent on the context and situation of the individual and their employer. Employers should remember that the duty and responsibility to ensure adjustments are made is on **them** - it's not the duty of an individual to know what they need. Once an employer is aware or could reasonably be expected to know that a person is disabled (for example, performance problems suggesting a disability), they have a legal duty to make reasonable adjustments.

It's sensible for employers to ring-fence a central budget for reasonable adjustments to ensure that cost is not a barrier to inclusion, as recommended by 'Legally Disabled?'.[16] This means managers can consider adjustments without having to consider various costing implications for the budget of their own team, and relieves the pressure of them 'working' in the ways that they are hoped to work - this is an ongoing, iterative process.

It's important to remember that adjustments are a collaborative experiment to understand what will work - they may need regular review and 'adjusting' over time. Employees should be made aware and reassured that the expectations of them and their performance do not change as a result of putting adjustments in place, as this could lead to anxiety - ironically lessening the effectiveness of support!

---

16   http://legallydisabled.com/wp-content/uploads/2020/01/Legally-Disabled-full-report-FINAL.pdf

Reasonable adjustments for ADHD

One of the most common questions I am asked is about what reasonable adjustments a person should ask for, because we often have no idea where to start.

An independent party such as an Occupational Health expert can help with this, who may have specialist knowledge of a condition such as ADHD and be able to help identify adjustments that can support a person in the workplace by making recommendations in a report. However, the individual will know themselves best and what will or will not work for them - they should always be involved in conversations about adjustments and given the choice of whether they should be adopted.

The below list is not exhaustive by any means, but these are some common examples of support that can help to not only level the playing field between ADHD and non-ADHD employees, but support us to thrive at work:

1) ADHD coaching

As in chapter 'Spotting ADHD at work', ADHD is associated with a 30% developmental delay in skills such as self-awareness, memory, impulsivity, motivation, emotional regulation and problem solving. Having a specialised coach who is trained in ADHD can help a person to strengthen these skills, understanding what strategies work specifically for them in relation to their ADHD.

As this is specifically tailored to ADHD, it can help reduce the substantial disadvantage ADHD employees may experience because of their condition at work, such as in relation to time management, organisation and communication. Coaching is also incredibly helpful to ensure other support and strategies are effective, as we can help to ensure someone actually implements them with extra ADHD-friendly accountability!

My job is to essentially work myself out of a job: coaching is designed for a time limited period to help someone implement the skills independently. It's like having someone standing in the kitchen with you whilst you do the washing up - without them there it's boring, but eventually the habit becomes routine. You might not do it perfectly for the rest of your life, but the habit and knowledge is embedded into your brain for when you need it.

ADHD Coaching can be funded by Access to Work in the UK, as explained in chapter 'Navigating Access to Work'. This is usually referred to as 'Workplace Strategy Coaching', and should be tailored to a person's specific ADHD needs.

2) Administrative support, task swapping, and/or changes to a job role / criteria

Having ADHD can feel like having a Ferrari brain with bicycle brakes, which means that we may find seemingly 'easy' tasks harder than traditionally 'hard' tasks. We can achieve a huge amount at work because of our ability to hyper focus, but it may be the repetitive, administrative tasks that we struggle most with.

Reallocating certain tasks or adjusting some aspects of a role can be a reasonable adjustment for employers to consider, including changing a job role entirely if required to redeploy a person within the organisation elsewhere. This might be relevant if they are struggling with certain tasks that are necessary for them to do their job, for example, but there are other jobs they could do within a company. This should also be built into criteria for progression and promotion, adapting criteria as may be needed for a person to progress to the next stage of their career.

I've coached many highly successful corporate professionals who have experienced very serious problems because of this, for example, in failing to submit tax returns on time, or filling in timesheets incorrectly. This can undermine all of our work, as we unconsciously self-sabotage our successes with failing to follow through - the first 80% of a task can feel much easier than the last 20%.

This is why administrative support can be so helpful for a person with ADHD. Having someone who can help me with the tasks I am simply unable to do, like setting up a zoom call, or submitting receipts properly, means I can do my job. Without this, none of ADHD Works would work!

In the workplace, this doesn't necessarily have to involve hiring a whole person to support with administration (though this can be funded by Access to Work as a support worker). Easy adjustments could be initiating 'task swaps' with employees who can support each other in certain areas, such as proof reading. This allows everybody to focus on their 'zone of genius', supporting each other with challenges, and fostering collective working.

Another reasonable adjustment within this may be to adapt the expectations or targets of an employee with ADHD, measuring their performance in alternative ways. For example, people with ADHD who are billed by the time worked, may benefit from an alternative way of measuring their success and performance. I could do a huge amount of work in a very short period of time such as writing a report, especially in comparison to my colleagues, but I would spend hours on tasks that would take them 5 minutes.

Employers can measure success by outputs and results, instead of what has traditionally been done. This is also applicable to roles involving billable hours, where a person may need to track their time, which a person with ADHD may significantly struggle with. Employers can make adjustments to adapt these targets as needed, otherwise their future career prospects may depend on targets that are much harder for them to meet than their colleagues. This is explained further in chapter 'ADHD Career Growth',

3) Written instructions and information

This is one of the easiest adjustments out there - simply *writing things down.* Many people with ADHD can struggle heavily with verbal and audio processing, in addition to memory challenges. Having all instructions and key information written down in ways that are clear and accessible to neurodivergent people can be incredibly helpful.

Personally, I used to create agendas for every single 1:1 catch up call I had at work. These helped me with anxiety and certainty, preparing what I was going to say beforehand instead of feeling overwhelmed with a blank memory. Ironically, everybody kept thanking me for sending them an agenda, saying how helpful it was and how they wished other people would do the same!

Having written agendas for meetings can be very useful to keep discussions on track in general, especially for neurodivergent people. As we can also struggle with Rejection Sensitive Dysphoria, providing written feedback can also be very helpful in providing processing time in advance of a discussion.

When requesting a meeting or 'quick chat' with an ADHD employee, I strongly recommend giving the context around this in writing, just explaining what you'd like to talk about, and providing reassurance that it's nothing bad. This small change can make a huge difference in our anxiety levels!

It's also strongly recommended to provide written records of adjustments that can be referred back to for everybody's sake, such as by creating an ADHD Action Plan, as in chapter 'Creating an ADHD Friendly Culture'. Providing written timelines and summaries can be very useful for people with ADHD to not have to second guess their own memories or ask for clarification later on.

In general, making procedures as simple & accessible as possible, such as by having written reasonable adjustments & sign-off policies, can also be extremely helpful.

4) Using SMART goals and briefing documents

A briefing document is simply written information about what work involves, that is collaboratively completed as a team at the outset of any new work or projects. This gives everybody the opportunity to ask questions and to set clear expectations and timeframes, alongside confirming sign-off processes - see chapter 'Managing ADHD for Success' for a template.

As an ADHD coach, I often do this with my clients, supporting them to put reminders in their calendar and think through various people they may need to check in with at certain times. This helps with the executive functioning challenges that people with ADHD can experience with planning ahead and breaking goals down into chunks, but also helps everybody in understanding exactly what is expected of them at work!

This can help to reduce siloed working and increase responsibility and ownership for teams, which I've found very useful in running ADHD Works. As my brain can speed ahead and create entire courses and books (like this one!) without always remembering to explain it to everybody that works with me, holding regular meetings to set out briefing documents for work means everyone is on the same page - literally!

Breaking down instructions into areas like 'what', 'who', 'when', and 'why' can be incredibly helpful, giving the context around instructions and making clear what has to happen. Setting up goals in a 'SMART' way can be highly effective. This means ensuring instructions are:

- Specific: what exactly is required of a person? Being very specific and clear about terms like 'research' is important here, as we may take things very literally.

- Measurable: how will we know when this is completed? At what point can we decide that something has been done?

- Achievable: is this realistic? The challenges with self-awareness linked to ADHD mean that we may automatically say yes, without taking time to consider everything that might be required to do this, in addition to all of our other work, and taking breaks!

- Relevant: what is the purpose of this work? As in chapter 'Managing ADHD for Success', this is very important for people with ADHD, as it helps to ignite our interest-based nervous system as opposed to simply being told to do something.

- Time-bound: when does this have to be done by, and what are time frames involved? It may be helpful to also establish when the work will actually take place here, such as breaking work down into different days and blocking this out on a calendar. This helps with the 'now or not now' way of thinking that can accompany ADHD!

5) ADHD training

As people with ADHD literally work differently to 'most' people, organisations can access training as a reasonable adjustment to ensure that they are not disadvantaged as a result of operating in neurotypical environments.

This could look like training for a person's organisation, manager, colleagues, or HR, for example. If the people around us understand that how we work is simply part of how our brains are wired, this fosters much more collaborative and effective working environments for everybody, as explained in chapter 'Creating an ADHD Friendly Culture'.

The relevance of this as a reasonable adjustment is that we may experience substantial disadvantages due to our ADHD in working with others that impact our ability to do our work. For example, if my colleagues hadn't been so receptive to my provision of agendas in advance of our meetings, this could have caused confusion and conflict between us.

As in chapter 'Managing ADHD for Success', providing training for managers of people with ADHD may also be extremely helpful in reducing or removing the substantial disadvantage they may experience because of thinking differently to 'most' people. Access to Work can help fund disability awareness training such as this, and co-coaching for an individual and their manager, to learn how to work most effectively together.

6) Communication and reassurance

The emotional regulation aspects of ADHD mean we may be liable to overthinking situations, such as ruminating on endless possible scenarios, and find it very difficult to ask for help or reassurance because of this.

This is particularly relevant for situations relating to potential rejection or mistakes being made, such as during a probation period or professional reviews. Certain adjustments can go a long way in helping to reduce this anxiety and supporting people to understand how to ask for help.

For example, managers could provide context for impromptu meetings, hold regular check ins and share positive feedback on an ongoing basis. Providing feedback in writing can be particularly helpful to give people time to process information.

It's also important to remember that people with ADHD may really struggle with communicating their needs on a day to day basis, so thinking ahead to support them with this can be very helpful. For example, if a person is permitted to work from home as a reasonable adjustment when needed, they may struggle with practically asking for this, feeling as though they are drawing attention to themselves or asking permission for something that has already been agreed.

Implementing adjustments in ways that accommodate for these communication challenges is very important, such as by agreeing that a person has the flexibility to decide on their working locations and can update their calendar as needed, instead of having to ask for permission each time.

Having a clear line of communication for people with ADHD to raise any concerns or ask questions, such as by offering a telephone check in prior to interview, or offering a 'mentor' in the workplace, can be extremely helpful, especially to prevent small issues turning into big ones.

Providing additional information and context in general can be very useful, especially for anything relating to their ADHD at work. For example, if an ADHD employee has a sick day and is asked whether this related to their disability, they may feel unsure, as ADHD itself is not an illness like the flu. The employee may feel awkward talking about this, but having an explanation and reassurance around the purpose of the question, such as an explanation that absences related to their ADHD do not count as absences for HR sickness policies, can be extremely helpful. It may even be possible to agree in advance, to some extent, how to identify this type of absence, such as burnout and anxiety symptoms versus other illnesses such as food poisoning.

7) Flexibility and trust

Above anything else, it's important that people with ADHD are trusted at work, with the flexibility to adapt their working environment to their needs. This could look like having flexible working location or times in place, for example.

Being trusted to take breaks or work from another location when needed, or to work the hours that suit us, without having to ask permission, is extremely helpful in giving neurodivergent people autonomy and control over their environments. The Covid-19 pandemic proved that it is possible for the majority of people to work from home, including doing their work (which may make it very difficult for any employer to then say such a change would not be a reasonable adjustment!).

For anyone, trusting them to get the work done in the ways that work best for them is the easiest way to see a dedicated, loyal, and highly effective employee.

8) Software and equipment

There's a variety of software, tools and equipment that can reduce disadvantages that people with ADHD experience at work. Our technological world is moving extremely fast, but essentially, any tools that can support us with alleviating certain disadvantages at work may be an appropriate adjustment.

For example, a standing desk or certain chair may be helpful for people with ADHD to have a working environment adapted to their needs, as we can struggle with having excess energy or needing to move around. For me, it would be extremely helpful to have duplicates of equipment such as laptop chargers in different places, as I am always forgetting mine!

Software that can help us with reminders and organisation, such as calendar reminders or vibrating digital watches, can also be extremely useful for challenges such as time management and organisation.

Dictation type software, such as turning speech to notes, is also a common adjustment which can be particularly helpful for people who struggle with taking notes and memory. I'm often having dictation software join coaching sessions! Further to this, artificial intelligence such as Chat GPT can also be extremely helpful, such as by helping to break down tasks into steps and provide reassurance on issues a person may be overthinking, such as how to sign off an email.

How can these adjustments support people with ADHD?

Ultimately, to make a reasonable adjustment for someone with ADHD, it's important to look at the **challenges** they are facing, which is why it can be helpful to have an external assessment from an expert who can facilitate this and provide recommendations of support.

Adjustments should be considered in the context of removing or reducing barriers to a disabled person being able to do their job like everybody else.

This will look different for everybody, but some examples are listed below. These are non-exhaustive, but it's worth focusing on a few key adjustments as needed in these sorts of discussions to ensure they can be effectively implemented. Many of these should hopefully be common practice in the workplace!

1. Executive Functioning Area: Self-awareness
Challenges that could arise:
Although differences in self-awareness can lead people with ADHD to do exceptional work of a very high quality, this can also result in a range of disadvantages to the individual, including:

• Burnout: mental and physical exhaustion and overworking
• Depression and/or anxiety
• Migraines
• Insomnia
• Eye twitches or other tics
• Posture-related pain e.g back, wrist, neck pain
• Weight gain or loss, poor nutrition and/or dehydration
• Bladder issues
• Experiencing sensory overwhelm without realising e.g unconsciously using excessive energy on attempting to focus despite distractions such as people talking or masking ADHD symptoms.
• Struggling to ask for help or realising that they need help!

Strategies for an individual to take:
This is a non-exhaustive list and will be dependent on the situation, but some examples of strategies that could be taken by an individual may include:

- Planning breaks and holidays in advance
- Taking a lunch break, with this blocked out in their calendar
- Having automatic replies on emails to block off time and focus as needed, and/or alert colleagues that they are at full capacity and cannot take on extra work
- Building in a weekly slot to review existing commitments for the week ahead and times to prioritise for rest and relaxation.
- Setting reminders to take breaks and check in with their posture and ensuring they use appropriate equipment e.g sitting in a desk chair instead of the sofa
- Doing exercise such as yoga to support with posture
- Deleting email apps from their phone so they only work in designated areas
- Using noise-cancelling headphones or ear plugs e.g Loop earplugs are excellent for those who experience noise sensitivities.

Reasonable adjustments employers could make:
This is a non-exhaustive list and will be dependent on the situation, but some examples of reasonable adjustments that could be made by an employer may include:

- Making referrals to independent experts such as Occupational Health to help identify support that may be needed for an individual if they are unsure

- Providing extra 1:1 catch ups and oversight to ensure an employee is not burning out
- Providing mentor and peer support
- Providing wellness support and education such as therapy or ADHD coaching
- Flexible working times / locations as needed
- Specific instructions with clear timeframes
- Supporting and encouraging employees to use automatic replies on emails as needed and to communicate that they cannot take on any extra requests
- Allowing employees to have breaks specified in their calendar as blocked out, so no meetings are booked during these periods.
- Providing specialist equipment such as seats or standing desks to enable an employee to work effectively and healthily.
- Providing specialist equipment such as a monitor screen
- Adapting environments as may be needed to avoid sensory overwhelm

2. Executive Functioning Area: Memory
Challenges that could arise:

Although differences in memory can result in people with ADHD being extremely resilient in 'bouncing back' from our challenges and focused on work, this can also result in a range of disadvantages to the individual, including:

- Forgetting information such as instructions or dates e.g performance reviews
- Difficulty organising belongings such as remembering keys and/or computer equipment
- Challenges remembering sequences involving many steps e.g sign-off procedures or IT processes
- Forgetting their successes and struggling to communicate these effectively when needed, potentially leading to a lack of career progression
- Struggling with meetings or presentations where impromptu memory recall is required (e.g interviews)
- Struggling with remembering necessary information for travel and office layouts, so potentially getting lost!

Strategies for an individual to take:
This is a non-exhaustive list and will be dependent on the situation, but some examples of strategies that could be taken by an individual may include:

- Using briefing documents for work when starting new projects, recording key dates and instructions to ensure these are ticked off as appropriate and shared with relevant colleagues.
- Using a reminder system such as digital reminders or relevant software

- Using written agendas for meetings where possible
- Taking notes to meetings / interviews / presentations as needed
- Using dictation or note-taking software
- Setting artificial deadlines for work with extra accountability
- Using visual reminders such as whiteboards or post-it notes
- Using 'tracker' software such as electronic geo-tags on belongings
- Using secure password software to store information in one place

Reasonable adjustments employers could make:
This is a non-exhaustive list and will be dependent on the situation, but some examples of reasonable adjustments that could be made by an employer may include:

- Providing and/or allowing employees to use software as needed e.g geo-tagging equipment, password software, dictation software.
- Using briefing documents for work to record instructions, relevant dates, and pre-plan meetings as needed
- Recording adjustments and additional information about support or important things of note e.g performance review dates in an ADHD Action Plan

- Providing written information and instructions in an accessible way e.g in a shared Google drive
- Providing a single desk to work from (e.g as opposed to 'hot desking')
- Providing additional equipment in case of some being forgotten e.g chargers
- Providing additional training as may be required e.g in relation to office layouts or sign-off processes
- Supporting employees with artificial deadlines and reminders as needed
- Reminding employees of priorities and important short-term goals as needed
- Providing additional 1:1 support such as manager check ins and/or coaching as a 'designed pause' to plan ahead and prioritise tasks.
- Allowing and encouraging visual reminders of work around the office e.g posters on walls, whiteboards.

3. Executive Functioning Area: Emotional Regulation

Challenges that could arise:

Although differences in emotional regulation can result in people with ADHD being extremely enthusiastic, loyal and compassionate towards others, this can also result in a range of disadvantages to the individual, including:

- Overwhelming emotional reactions e.g experiencing 'Rejection Sensitive Dysphoria' as set out in chapter 'Spotting ADHD at Work'
- Struggling to communicate with others and to process feedback, especially without time to prepare for this.
- Experiencing anxiety, panic attacks and stress, especially around performance and related periods such as probation or conflict.
- Ruminating over 'small' decisions such as what to wear, when to take a break, eat lunch, or how to sign off an email.
- Using excessive energy in 'masking' their symptoms, such as withdrawing from sharing their ideas or social events such as team lunches, particularly if they do not feel psychologically safe at work.
- Finding it difficult to ask for help or promote themselves or their work e.g in performance review meetings where they may be experiencing stress.
- Feeling anxious about taking time off when unwell or how to follow official procedures if they are not sure what should happen next, such as disclosing ADHD or requesting holiday - resulting in struggles meeting their own needs or doing these things.
- Finding it difficult to advocate for themselves as needed.

Strategies for an individual to take:

This is a non-exhaustive list and will be dependent on the situation, but some examples of strategies that could be taken by an individual may include:

- Seeing a therapist and ADHD coach to learn emotional regulation strategies and process emotions effectively
- Taking breaks as needed e.g exercising when feeling overwhelmed
- Seeking a buddy or mentor to provide reassurance for 'quick questions' such as how to sign off an email or what's 'normal'.
- Using software such as ChatGPT to help with rumination e.g by accessing perspective on situations, and in providing templates for things such as emails and communication. (I use this a lot!)
- Noting down their successes on a regular basis and sharing these regularly e.g with a manager and/or providing these in advance of meetings related to career progression
- Identifying ways that work for them to help with anxiety, known as 'stimming' e.g by using a fidget toy, jewellery, making notes, wearing noise-cancelling headphones, and/or listening to music, to name a few!

- Identifying situations in advance that may result in emotional regulation challenges and accessing support as needed e.g from a colleague who is a wellbeing / ADHD Champion, and/or planning in time to process emotions.

Reasonable adjustments employers could make:
This is a non-exhaustive list and will be dependent on the situation, but some examples of reasonable adjustments that could be made by an employer may include:

- Allowing employees to work from locations such as home or to take breaks when needed without having to ask for permission each time, and making the process of how they do this clear e.g in an ADHD Action Plan
- Providing training for employees, particularly managers, on management techniques specific to ADHD and ensuring all employees are properly trained in company processes e.g disability policies
- Identifying sources of stress and making adjustments as needed e.g by changing a person's line manager if their relationship is incompatible, or adapting their role as may be required.
- Labelling meetings with brief explanations and context (and training managers / colleagues to do so!)

- Providing information such as interview questions or feedback in advance of meetings
- Encouraging and accepting information as may be relevant in alternative formats e.g an employee providing their 'wins' in writing prior to a performance meeting.
- Providing clearly defined and recorded 'SMART' expectations for employees to meet, especially in relation to performance.
- Allowing employees to 'stim' as needed to regulate themselves e.g by using a fidget toy in meetings or taking notes
- Providing employees with buddies or mentors to support each other
- Providing wellness support such as therapy and/or software such as Unmind (a workplace wellbeing platform)
- Providing options for social events e.g hybrid online / in person events to ensure they are accessible to everybody
- Allowing and encouraging a range of opportunities for employees to communicate such as to ask for help, engage in meetings, or provide feedback e.g through an anonymous helpline
- Allowing an employee to access support from others where may be needed e.g by bringing another colleague / support worker to a meeting that induces a lot of stress.

4. Executive Functioning Area: Problem Solving
Challenges that could arise:
Although differences in problem solving can result in highly valuable qualities of innovation and creative thinking from people with ADHD, this can also result in a range of disadvantages to the individual, including:

- Making decisions, prioritising information, and breaking tasks down.
- Experiencing overwhelm and struggling to delegate to others, resulting in potential misunderstandings or conflict.
- Difficulty managing their own workloads or the workloads of others.
- Time management and working at paces that others do not, such as getting things done very quickly! We may perceive time as 'now' or 'not now'.
- Following highly bureaucratic or detailed procedures involving many steps e.g sign-off processes involving many people.
- Having lots of brilliant ideas which may challenge the status quo, which may result in misunderstandings or frustration, especially if these are not necessarily related to their specific job description or in environments that are not open to change.

Strategies for an individual to take:

This is a non-exhaustive list and will be dependent on the situation, but some examples of strategies that could be taken by an individual may include:

- Having ADHD coaching to implement ADHD-friendly strategies and systems to break down tasks and work in a sustainable way for ourselves and others.
- Having routines such as a regular 'stand up' meeting with colleagues or objective to prioritise goals and actions for the day, with extra account-ability.
- Regularly reviewing workloads with managers and colleagues to ensure tasks are broken down and prioritised effectively, with clear responsibility set out for each area.
- Asking for 'SMART' goals and using Briefing Documents for projects to record this in one place.
- Writing out important written instructions or processes and making these visible e.g by using a whiteboard as a reminder to follow sign-off processes.
- Identifying when the 'end' point is when starting any work: how will they know if it's finished? What happens after this point?
- Setting reminders and artificial deadlines for time management

Reasonable adjustments employers could make:
This is a non-exhaustive list and will be dependent on the situation, but some examples of reasonable adjustments that could be made by an employer may include:

- Providing neurodiversity-friendly training or coaching for ADHD employees e.g on management
- Providing ADHD training for teams to provide context for differing styles of working.
- Providing or supporting additional meetings for an employee to set goals and hold themselves accountable, e.g by having a regular 1:1 meeting with their manager each week to do this or having daily 'stand up' meetings for teams to do this collectively.
- Ensuring employees use Briefing Documents and/or SMART goals when setting out work and projects, and that 'end points' are always set for tasks.
- Signposting towards and providing reminders about important information or processes such as sign-off procedures e.g by providing a physical employee 'manual'.
- Adjusting job roles or tasks as many be relevant e.g adjusting the number of people that an ADHD employee manages, if needed.

- Upholding artificial deadlines where relevant.
- Providing relevant software e.g organisational tools.

5. Executive Functioning Area: Motivation
Challenges that could arise:

Although differences in motivation can result in extraordinary results in the workplace from people with ADHD in being able to 'hyper-focus' on their work and work to a very fast pace, this can also result in a range of disadvantages to the individual, including:

- Procrastination & struggling to start or finish tasks that are not of interest
- Becoming easily distracted and finding it difficult to concentrate e.g in environments such as offices - although some people with ADHD may need environments like this to concentrate!
- Struggling to multi-task - or struggling to do 1 thing at a time!
- Burnout (and those challenges listed in 'Self-awareness', such as not taking breaks).
- Struggling excessively with certain tasks e.g those involving repetitive tasks, such as administration, but being able to do others extremely well. This can make it difficult to explain or ask for help and lead to a person questioning themselves.
- Only being able to focus at certain times or in certain locations e.g late at night.

Strategies for an individual to take:
This is a non-exhaustive list and will be dependent on the situation, but some examples of strategies that could be taken by an individual may include:

- Having ADHD coaching to understand how their 'interest based nervous system' works and strategies to apply to challenging tasks.
- 'Gamifying' these tasks e.g setting a daily challenge to complete
- 'Body doubling' - working alongside a person to get work done for extra accountability. There's also a range of ways of doing this online such as FocusMate.
- Identifying methods that work for focus and motivation e.g working hours or locations and communicating these to others.
- Using noise cancelling headphones / earplugs
- Administrative support or task swapping with colleagues
- Preparing for distractions in advance e.g by blocking certain websites or putting distractions like phones out of sight
- Using the 'Pomodoro technique' to focus: working for 20 minutes with a 5 minute break
- Using visual timers and having clocks centrally located!
- Blocking out work on a calendar in advance, including setting and sticking to working hours.

Reasonable adjustments employers could make:

This is a non-exhaustive list and will be dependent on the situation, but some examples of reasonable adjustments that could be made by an employer may include:

- Providing tailored support such as ADHD coaching, administrative support or assistance from colleagues
- Allowing and encouraging teams to 'task swap' and share responsibilities as works best for them
- Providing extra 1:1 sessions and accountability for employees
- Providing software or equipment as may be needed e.g noise-cancelling headphones
- Allowing flexible working hours and locations, and providing quiet areas to work in.
- Providing management training to understand how to best motivate ADHD employees.

6. Executive Functioning Area: Inhibition / Impulsivity

Challenges that could arise:

Although differences in inhibition can result in brilliant ideas and non-linear thinking from employees with ADHD, this can also result in a range of disadvantages to the individual, including:

- Communication challenges, such as interrupting colleagues
- Talking about topics or ideas at times where the focus is agreed to be on something else, which can result in anxiety and misunderstandings.
- Becoming distracted during conversations and work (as in 'Motivation')
- Finding it difficult to stick to decisions or plans.
- Doing work without communicating this to colleagues in advance.
- Having lots of ideas and being able to spot improvements that could be made, but feeling disillusioned if these are not taken on.
- Accidentally doing other people's work for them, or saying yes to requests without thinking this through (as in 'Self-awareness').

Strategies for an individual to take:
This is a non-exhaustive list and will be dependent on the situation, but some examples of strategies that could be taken by an individual may include:

- Creating agendas before meetings (and using them!), or asking for subject specific meetings.
- Setting short term goals such as weekly and daily objectives
- Exercising and using up our energy!

- Stimming such as with a fidget toy or writing notes in order to concentrate
- Using Briefing Documents and/or SMART goals to delegate tasks to others, setting out clear responsibility and setting ourselves reminders not to do them!
- Writing new ideas down before acting upon them (or emailing them to ourselves!) and having a designated 'pause' to review these such as by having weekly ADHD coaching.
- Asking for clear expectations and tasks to be broken down into short term goals.

Reasonable adjustments employers could make:
This is a non-exhaustive list and will be dependent on the situation, but some examples of reasonable adjustments that could be made by an employer may include:

- Holding subject specific meetings, with agendas provided beforehand
- Designating an opportunity for 'blue sky' ideas to be shared e.g a monthly meeting where employees can present their ideas and a process for these to be considered.
- Providing clearly written instructions and procedures, ensuring employees fully under- stand these and the purpose behind them.

- Allowing employees to 'stim' or fidget as needed
- Providing additional training and/or coaching on ADHD-friendly delegation and management styles.
- Having a mentor or buddy system

How to ask for adjustments if you have ADHD

Asking for help at work for your ADHD can be an extremely vulnerable thing to do, but it can also be extremely helpful. It's understandably very anxiety-inducing, especially because of the risk of this being ignored or denied, and having to decide what to do next.

The legalities and formalities involved in reasonable adjustments and disability can feel scary, and difficult to get the balance right of 'officially' asking for help without worrying about your employer thinking you're threatening them! Their response is not your responsibility, and most employers should hopefully be receptive and supportive to having conversations about this.

It can also feel scary to actually be granted this support, because we might feel additional pressure on us as a result, and it may not work as we hope. Again, this is not your burden to carry: reasonable adjustments might sound official and final, but they are really an iterative, continuous process of ensuring you are supported as needed at work. If they don't work as hoped, there are endless other options - this doesn't necessarily mean you can't do your job!

You also don't need to know what support or adjustments you'd like to have in place, as the duty to ensure these are made is on your employer. If you do know, remember that what you want may not always be provided exactly as requested, and there may be certain time-delays involved, as an employer may need to follow certain processes to ensure they are upholding their legal obligations. This can feel very stressful, but it doesn't mean that you're not being supported!

Overall, it's vitally important that you are treated with respect and dignity at work throughout, and feel safe enough to seek support where needed.

As it can feel very overwhelming figuring out how to ask for reasonable adjustments, you may wish to complete the following table to identify what you need. Using the Executive Functioning quiz from chapter 'Spotting ADHD at Work' may be very helpful for this.

Providing this much context isn't necessary, but it can help us to feel more confident and reassured in identifying our needs and reassuring ourselves that we're doing the best we can with what we have available to us.

Template to ask for adjustments

Once you have established the adjustments that could help you at work, you may wish to ask your employer for help! If helpful, you can use and adapt the below template as needed.

Dear [Manager / HR Colleague Name]

As you know / I wanted to let you know that I have Attention Deficit Hyperactivity Disorder, which I feel is a disability because of the substantial and long-term negative effect it has on my ability to carry out normal day to day activities.

I have been learning more about the challenges I experience at work because of my ADHD, which has enabled me to identify changes that could be implemented to help remove or reduce these disadvantages.

I would like to please request the following reasonable adjustments from you as my employer to support me with ADHD at work:

As I can struggle to... *[insert challenge, e.g understand my own needs]*, **this results in...** *[insert effect e.g take on too much work and burning out]*.

I am already... *[insert what you are doing e.g using my calendar to time block work]*.. **but I need further help from you as my employer to support me with this.**

[If you know what adjustment to ask for…]

A reasonable adjustment that could be made to support me with this is… *[insert adjustment e.g have weekly check ins with my manager and for them to help me ensure I am not saying yes to new work].*

This will help… *[insert how it will reduce the disadvantage e.g ensure I have an objective view on my workload and ensure I can provide high quality work at a sustainable level, without burning out.]*

I am also happy to discuss any additional adjustments or support that may be helpful, as I am very keen to ensure I can work to the best of my abilities.

I would be grateful if you could please let me know next steps and timeframes.

Thank you very much in advance for your support.

Best wishes,

[Your Name]

ADHD Challenge	How this disadvantages me at work	Things I am already doing	Reasonable adjustments that could be made	How this will reduce the disadvantage
e.g memory	e.g struggling to remember instructions	e.g setting up calendar reminders	e.g providing written information and instructions, using briefing documents for work	e.g can follow instructions and meet expectations effectively
e.g emotional regulation / Rejection Sensitive Dysphoria	e.g finding it difficult to ask for help, anxiety around distractions or impromptu meetings	e.g seeing a therapist	e.g having the ability to work from home when needed, having context for meetings in advance	e.g can self-regulate as needed, concentrate as needed without distractions
e.g becoming distracted in the office, struggling to focus due to impulsivity and self-awareness	e.g struggling to concentrate on work or say no to requests / conversations	e.g using noise cancelling headphones	e.g flexible working times and locations	e.g can concentrate on work without distractions as needed
e.g administrative and repetitive tasks, motivation and procrastination, needing challenge and stimulation from work	e.g struggling to complete these tasks, spending an extremely long time on them or doing them incorrectly e.g setting up meetings, resulting in very high stress	e.g asking colleagues for help	e.g task swapping so the responsibility for these tasks lies with a colleague, and/or administrative support	e.g reduce stress levels and can concentrate on other areas of work that do not have these challenges

Template: Workplace Adjustment Agreement

After reasonable adjustments have been agreed, they should be recorded in writing and made accessible to the individual they are about. The below Workplace Adjustment Agreement template may be useful to do this.

This is a record of the reasonable adjustments agreed to support [name]. This agreement may be reviewed and amended as necessary with the agreement of [name] and their line manager.

Regular review sessions have been scheduled as agreed at: [relevant dates]

Individual:

I have: _____

This may impact me at work in the following ways: _____

The reasonable adjustments that have been agreed to support me are: _____

Anything else relevant to note (e.g referrals that have been made): _____

Date adjustments agreed: _____

Date adjustments implemented (if relevant): _____

The dates this Agreement will be reviewed are: _____

My point of contact for this is: _____

Any other individuals who will be or are aware of these adjust-ments are: _____

Individual's signature: _____
Date: _____

Employer's signature: _____
Date: _____

Chapter 6
Navigating Access to Work

Access to Work is like the rainbow at the end of the painfully expensive journey of navigating ADHD. However, like a rainbow, it can be very hard to actually get to, even when we can see it in the distance!

This scheme can be very complex and bureaucratic, but it can be extremely helpful if you can navigate it. It's applicable to any health condition impacting a person at work, and at the time of writing, there's up to £66,000 worth of funding available per person, per year. Although this sounds like a lot of money, the support provided will be awarded depending on the needs of a person, and there's a strong focus on cost-effectiveness - so it will be different for each individual.

It's important to note that like everything in this book, this information is correct to the best of my abilities and knowledge at the time of writing, and is based off my personal experiences as opposed to formal advice to be relied upon. It's strongly advisable to look at the most up to date information online, *especially* with ATW, as it can be a very complicated system that changes quickly. This can be found on the gov.uk website or by contacting Access to Work directly.[17]

What is Access to Work (ATW)?

This is a Government grant scheme that helps fund support for anybody with a health condition impacting them at work, with the aim of supporting them to stay in work. This health condition doesn't necessarily have to be a disability, it just has to be a 'physical or mental health condition or disability that means you need support to do your job or get to and from work'.

A person needs to be 16 years old or older, and to live and work (or be about to start or return to work) in England, Scotland, or Wales. There's a different system in Northern Ireland[18], and this scheme doesn't apply to people living in the Channel Islands or the Isle of Man.

This work must be paid, and includes people who are self-employed, Directors of companies, and people doing apprenticeships. However, Access to Work does not cover people who work in the Civil

---

17 https://www.gov.uk/access-to-work
18 https://www.nidirect.gov.uk/articles/employment-support-information

Service, because there's another system in place where employers provide this support directly. ATW applications can be made up to 6 weeks before an individual starts a new job, or after they have started.

Although a formal medical diagnosis is not required for an ATW grant, it's important to note that ATW do not provide medical support, such as diagnostic assessments. An employer may wish to fund or contribute towards a medical assessment for an individual, which can be extremely helpful, especially as the waiting lists for ADHD assessments are so long in the UK.

As in 'Disclosing ADHD at Work' an employee will need to put contact details down for their employer when applying for ATW. This can cause various complications set out below, which employers should take particular care with, especially to avoid inadvertent discrimination:

1) Lack of awareness, understanding around or engagement with the processes

I have worked with several people who have unfortunately been met with dubious treatment as a result of enquiring about ATW with their employers. As many employers are unaware that this exists, and it sounds 'too good to be true', they might ask the employee to search for more information to 'prove' that they can apply, for example. Understandably, this can cause a lot of pressure and anxiety for the individual.

Technically, an employee doesn't need their employer's *permission* to apply for ATW, however, on a practical level, they do need their engagement. When a person applies to ATW, their employer is informed about the application and asked to confirm their employment and role within the company. They may also be asked whether they consent to cost-sharing, if support where this is relevant (e.g equipment) is granted.

This is primarily for administrative purposes, as opposed to being involved in the details of the assessment or support. Once this confirmation is provided, the process is handled by ATW and the individual. Depending on the support awarded, an employer may be asked to pay for this by the employee, and reclaim it back on their behalf.

However, if an employer is unaware about or does not trust any of the above, they may refuse to engage with the process. This may also be due to simply not having processes in place and bureaucracy. ATW sometimes have strict timelines to work with, so caseworkers may need confirmation and a response within a certain period of time to keep a case open. This means that employees may need to chase up their employer, which can feel quite stressful and embarrassing!

Supporting a person to apply for ATW could be considered a reasonable adjustment, depending on the situation, so it's highly recommended that employers have specific training on this and familiarise themselves with the process. The burden shouldn't be put on the employees to prove anything about ATW and they shouldn't be victimised as a result of applying!

If an employer does not wish to pay for the support, an individual may fund this themselves and reclaim it back (as happens with self-employed people, for example). This may not always be possible for individuals on a practical level, and so having the support of their employer is important in enabling them to access the support they need.

2) Lack of clear structure or process, such as contact details to provide in applications

If an employer is unaware about ATW, they may not know how to support an employee looking to apply for the scheme. For example, if an employee asks their manager whose contact details they should put down to confirm their employment, they may not know. Taking a common sense approach, this would usually be the same people who would confirm employment status to referencing services, such as rental agencies, like HR.

An employer can simplify this process by centralising and documenting the processes in an accessible location, such as on an intranet. Encouraging and supporting employees to apply for ATW is sensible, as they will be able to access support above and beyond that which is legally required, supporting them to do their jobs to the very best of their abilities. ATW can also fund training for employers such as disability impact or awareness training, in addition to coaching for managers and teams, which benefits everybody, as explained in chapter 'Creating an ADHD Friendly Culture'.

As this is also relevant to any health condition (regardless of whether this is a disability in law), such as anxiety, chronic fatigue, depression, or long Covid, ATW is an extraordinarily helpful source of support for employers and employees alike.

3) Confusion between reasonable adjustments and ATW support

ATW will not pay for reasonable adjustments or support that would be legally required at law. For example, if a person required wheelchair accessible entrances to enter their office, this would be a reasonable adjustment legally required under the Equality Act that an employer must cover.

In contrast, ATW can fund support *above and beyond reasonable adjustments*. This is complex, because the ATW process mostly involves conversations with the individual concerned, as opposed to an employer. The ATW website currently states that they will 'advise your employer if changes should be made as reasonable adjustments',[19] but they do not do assessments as an Occupational Health expert would, in making recommendations for employers to follow such as by providing flexible working times.

From my understanding, the focus is mainly on providing extra support for an individual, as opposed to supporting an employer on understanding how to meet their legal obligations.

This means that an employee applying for ATW does *not* discharge an employer's legal obligations to provide adjustments: it is not a replacement. If an employer becomes aware of a potential disability such as ADHD because of being notified about an ATW application, the same processes should be followed as though the individual was disclosing ADHD without this context. They may not necessarily need or want support from an employer at that point, but the processes should still be followed in line with their wishes.

Unfortunately, ATW applications can take a long time to process once a person has applied. At the time of writing, the waiting time is 6 months long. This means that although a person may not want support initially, for example, they may discover things later on during or after this waiting period that would be helpful to have in place as a reasonable adjustment.

---

19 https://www.gov.uk/access-to-work

They may understandably feel nervous about raising this, especially if they have already told an employer that they don't require any adjustments from them, so reassurance and easy methods of communication should be provided in case they later change their mind.

A person may have a workplace assessment as part of their ATW award, but this does not usually make suggestions for reasonable adjustments - this is purely focused on ATW support. Confusingly, some of these awards could potentially be considered a reasonable adjustment if they would reduce or remove the significant disadvantage a person experiences at work because of their disability, but ultimately only a tribunal would be able to confirm this.

So, this process does not replace any Occupational Health assessments which would typically provide a report of recommendations for adjustments to an employer and employee.

4) Confusion around payments and communication
Once opened, the ATW application process can be complicated, involving various conversations with ATW caseworkers and workplace assessors, resulting in a report setting out an individual's award.

During this application process, there may be inconsistencies and confusion, especially in relation to communications between ATW caseworkers, workplace assessors, employers, and employees. I spend a great deal of my time as an ADHD Coach helping people to navigate this, such as by referencing the ATW Caseworker Guidance to confirm the processes that should be followed. Understandably, this can be confusing for everyone as a result.

The grant isn't means tested, so it's awarded regardless of how much a person earns or has in savings. This being said, there may be scenarios where an employer may be asked to contribute towards costs for support including special aids and equipment, and adaptations to premises or equipment.

Cost-sharing doesn't apply to awards for support workers, such as administrative support, coaching, or training. Where it does apply, this is subject to certain thresholds depending on the number of employees within an organisation and total amount awarded.[20]

In my experience, the majority of ATW awards I have seen have provided support such as coaching, administrative support, software, and tools such as whiteboards or electronic readers. Personally, I have seen very few cases where an employer is expected to cost share, or where there have been awards where this may be required, such as relating to adaptations for an office.

---

20 https://www.gov.uk/government/publications/access-to-work-guide-for-employers/access-to-work-factsheet-for-employers

Employers will often pay for the support that is awarded and claim the money for this back from ATW directly. This is because after making an award, ATW will usually require the support to be purchased and to have taken place before paying for this. For an individual, this can be very difficult if they don't have the money in the first place!

There's a range of ways to do this, including postal forms and via an online portal. Individuals should not have pressure placed on them around this confusion - it's not their fault!

It is also important for employers to remember that this support is not them 'paying' to support an individual - the money is reclaimable. It should not be the case that this is viewed as 'special treatment', or that any special expectations are placed on an employee as a result of supporting them to access this assistance.

Instead, employees should be helped to actually make the most of this support, such as by making reasonable adjustments to allow them time to use it. For example, an individual may need to have a coaching call during their working hours, which could be a reasonable adjustment.

ATW can be very complicated for employers to understand where their responsibility lies, but ultimately, they can take a practical approach and work with this support to help their employees perform to the best of their abilities.

What is the ATW process?

Initially, an application needs to be made, which is usually done online, or can be completed over the phone. This should take approximately 15-30 minutes, and involves questions such as relating to the condition a person has and how this shows up for them at work. No medical documents are required, and a person doesn't have to know in advance what support would help them, as ATW can do a workplace assessment to help establish this. There's a free course helping people to apply for Access to Work on www.adhdworks.info.

When the application has been processed (most likely, a few months later), a caseworker from ATW will contact the individual and if they are employed, their employer, to confirm their employment details.

If the person knows what support they want, this process may be fairly straight forward. For example, they may tell their caseworker that they'd like to have coaching with a particular provider, and an award for this may be granted.

If they are not sure what support they need, or a caseworker feels it would be beneficial, a workplace assessment may be arranged to help establish what support may be helpful and for recommendations of support to be made for the ATW award. This could happen at a person's workplace, but is often held remotely, either via video call or telephone. This assessment should consist of a conversation lasting approximately 1 hour or less, focused on the types of support that could help a person to overcome any workplace challenges they may be experiencing with their health condition.

After this, the assessor will provide recommendations of support back to the ATW caseworker, who may discuss these with the individual. For support such as coaching or a support worker like a virtual assistant, an individual may be asked to find 3 quotes from different providers, or ATW may provide these themselves. Once the decision is made, a final report is posted to the applicant setting out the terms of their award and how they can ask for this decision to be reconsidered if they are not happy with it.

Overall, it's important that the support is **tailored to the individual's needs.** My first award from ATW was for a coaching provider whose website was focused on Dyslexia, which I was obviously very upset at, as I am not Dyslexic! I requested a reconsideration which was successful and allowed me to access the life changing ADHD coaching I needed.

When the support allocation has been used, an individual can apply for a renewal online.[21] This may result in an email or phone conversation with their caseworker, who can adapt their award as needed, suggest a new workplace assessment, or advise them to apply again. You can also apply again if your job situation changes during this period, for example, such as becoming self-employed.

What kind of support can be awarded through ATW?

ATW can fund a variety of different support, much of which may be similar to reasonable adjustments, but should *not* replace them. The support must help a person to stay in work, and should be cost effective.

The support should be focused on the context of the workplace. Mental health support is available by applying directly to one of the ATW providers set out on their website.[22]

For an ADHD-er, types of support awarded through ATW may include:

ADHD Workplace Coaching

This is generally referred to as 'workplace strategy coaching', because the coaching should be focused

---

21   https://www.gov.uk/access-to-work/renew
22   This is set out on the ATW website: https://www.gov.uk/access-to-work. At the time of writing, providers include Able Futures: https://able-futures.co.uk/individuals & Maximus: https://atw.maximusuk.co.uk

on supporting an individual to learn and implement strategies to support them at work.

In my experience, it's important that this coaching is specifically tailored to ADHD, as being neurodivergent means we think differently to 'most' people. Telling someone to try time management isn't going to work - we need support adapted to our needs!

This coaching can be for an individual, but it can also be awarded as 'co-coaching', which would involve an individual and their manager, for example. This can be helpful to understand how to work most effectively together. Coaching may also be awarded specifically for a person's manager.

If a person has already identified a coach that they would like to work with, they may request this directly from ATW and explain the context around this, providing quotes in advance.

Administrative / Other Assistant (Support Worker)

This is typically referred to as a 'support worker' by ATW, which is usually related to administration. For example, a virtual assistant, who could support a person to do their job with ADHD. ADHD Works wouldn't exist if this support hadn't been awarded to me - it can make a huge difference in enabling us to have support tailored to our specific ADHD challenges on an ongoing basis.

I've also seen support workers be awarded for contexts such as note taking, which can be very helpful for people with ADHD at work. It may be difficult to be awarded a support worker, as this is generally provided for an ongoing period of time, which means ongoing cost, as opposed to support that 'tailors off' such as coaching or a one time cost such as software.

However, it can be very much needed to support people with ADHD to do their jobs, and this will be situation dependent. For example, ATW may suggest trying alternative options such as software prior to being awarded a support worker.

Software

ATW often suggests software for people with ADHD such as technology based support, and may fund subscriptions to this. There are a huge range of options, which are typically directed by the individual or the assessor.

Some examples of software I've seen being awarded include:

- Body doubling apps and software, where a person can work alongside another person online

- Audio software, where a person can listen to material instead of reading it, for example

- Dictation software, where a person can record notes.

- Organisational software, such as calendar management and planners

- Note taking and storage software

- Courses and education: such as our range of ADHD Works courses, like 'ADHD at Work' and 'ADHD Champions' to train people in supporting their colleagues with ADHD at work.

   This kind of software can be very helpful, but not so much if we don't actually use it! This is why it's important to have coaching in place to ensure we learn the strategies to actually make use of the support awarded to us.

Equipment

Physical equipment and tools may also be suggested by ATW to support a person at work. This could include things like:

- Standing desks, supporting people who struggle to sit down and work

- Chairs that enable a person to change positions or support them with posture if they sit in unusual positions because of their ADHD (like me!)

- Laptop stands, supporting someone to work from different locations

- Laptops and computers, which could be tailored to the needs of a person with ADHD. I've had many coaching sessions with people via their phones, as they don't have a computer!

- Display monitors, which could help people to work from different screens and have everything in one place for them to see, instead of working from a small laptop with lots of tabs open, for example.

- Noise cancelling earplugs, which can be very helpful to enable us to focus. There are some which can be fit inside the ear, reducing but not removing completely the sounds around us, which can be very helpful for sensory issues.

- Headphones, which may help a person to work on the move and focus by listening to music whilst working, for example. Wireless headphones may be very helpful, especially if they include GPS tracking!

- Electronic tags for items, which can help a person to keep track of their belongings.

- Whiteboards, which can help with visual reminders and places to keep notes.

- Wall planners, which can be very useful for people with ADHD to keep track of their commitments and as a visual reminder to think ahead.

- Clocks, timers, and watches, which can all be very helpful for people with ADHD to keep track of time! Having visual egg timers that count down can support us with concentrating on work for short periods of time, for example, and reminders from digital watches that vibrate can also be extremely useful.

- Electronic notebooks, which can be very helpful to store and process all of our information and notes for work.

Again, this type of support can be very useful, but it's important to ensure that we will actually use it!

Training
ATW can fund ADHD awareness training for teams and organisations, which can be extremely helpful, as explained in chapter 'Creating an ADHD Friendly Culture'.

In general, training for managers, teams, and HR is incredibly helpful to understand how to best support neurodivergent employees.

Travel

A person may be awarded support relating to travel, if this is something they struggle with. For example, instead of living over the road from my job, I could have maybe accessed support for taxis to help me get to work without having numerous panic attacks on public transport!

Ultimately, ATW can fund support in a variety of innovative ways tailored to a person's specific health condition and challenges. It's an incredible way of accessing support that may otherwise be too expensive, impractical, or simply not known about.

Chapter 7
Resolving Workplace Challenges

There are many situations where ADHD may become relevant at work as a result of challenges. In an ideal world, an inclusive and supportive culture would be in place to prevent these challenges from happening in the first place, but it's important to recognise that this doesn't always happen.

Although there are legal safeguards protecting people from discrimination at work because of having ADHD, using these should be a last resort. I cannot emphasise the importance of trying to resolve issues as swiftly and informally as possible. Escalating workplace challenges and conflict into official reviews and procedures, is a huge waste of time and energy for both an employer and employee, and it can seriously impact the health and energy of everybody involved.

This being said, an individual with ADHD experiencing unfair treatment and being denied the support they need, especially in combination with the natural sense of social justice[23] that accompanies ADHD, can be all-consuming and debilitating to live with. Everybody deserves to be supported at work, regardless of disability, and the law exists for a reason: to ensure this happens.

Below are some examples of workplace challenges and conflicts that may arise in relation to ADHD, in addition to those already covered in previous chapters such as 'Disclosing ADHD at work' and 'Navigating Access to Work'. Like everything in this book, these are my own personal suggestions and shouldn't be relied upon, especially as legal advice - every situation will be highly individual and is the responsibility of those involved.

Above all, if you're not sure on any of this, or are experiencing challenges relating to your ADHD at work, I strongly recommend talking to an employment lawyer who can help you to understand your rights depending on your situation. Many will offer a free conversation at first to help you establish this. I would recommend finding a lawyer who operates on a fixed fee basis, in case you decide to go ahead with them, to avoid legal fees racking up.[24]

If you're an employee, I also strongly recommend joining an employee union as soon as you can - don't

---

23 https://edgefoundation.org/the-fairness-imperative-adhd-and-justice-sensitivity/
24 I'd recommend YESS Law https://www.yesslaw.org.uk, Tom Haines of InHouse it Legal Solutions https://inhouseit.co.uk or Sonay Erten https://www.legalstudio.co.uk/team/sonay-erten/ for this kind of work.

leave it until there's a problem! Some of these can support you in case of challenges as set out below and may be able to provide legal assistance.

Disclosure of ADHD being ignored

As explained in chapter, 'Disclosing ADHD at Work', disclosing ADHD at work is not always straightforward, especially if there's no processes in place to be followed. People may have different understandings of whether ADHD has been disclosed in the sense of triggering legal duties under the Equality Act for an employer to follow, and unaware of what they should do next.

This is especially so if people with ADHD mention it in passing, such as waiting to causally drop it into conversation and see the response. This is normal, because writing a formal email to officially 'disclose your disability', especially if you're not even sure if you have one, can feel extremely intimidating. Even if you do not have a formal diagnosis, for example, if you're awaiting a diagnosis, it's still important to disclose your concerns, as you may still be offered protection under the Equality Act.

They may also be unsure as to who counts as their employer, or what they need to do. For example, an employee may tell their colleague they have ADHD, but not their manager. Employers can make this simple by setting it out in a process, expanding upon the concept of 'disclosure' and how this can happen.

As the legal duty is on employers to make adjustments as soon as they are aware or could reasonably be expected to be aware that an employee has a disability, I believe that they should err on the side of caution and take all discussions of a person's health condition in the workplace very seriously, offering support and follow up conversations where needed.

For an individual, if you'd like your employer to be aware of your ADHD in the sense of ensuring you will be fully supported under the Equality Act, you may wish to make explicitly clear that you are disclosing ADHD in this context and consider it to be a disability. In general, it's advisable to ensure any disclosure is made to a manager, as opposed to a peer, and in writing, to avoid confusion around whether your company was aware or not. In an ideal world, you could tell them what you wanted to happen next, or the purpose behind telling them.

Initial responses to requests for reasonable adjustments

Asking for reasonable adjustments or support can be an extremely stressful and overwhelming experience, as explained in chapter 'Reasonable Adjustments for ADHD'. What happens next is highly dependent on the situation and individuals, but given the vulnerability and sensitivity involved, this can easily result in conflict and confusion.

In an ideal scenario, the process of requesting reasonable adjustments should be clarified within a policy. Ideally, a person shouldn't have to resort to formally requesting this in writing, having to spell out that they are requesting a reasonable adjustment to support them with their disability, but it might be clearer to do so for the avoidance of doubt.

Reasonable adjustments are spoken about here in the context of ADHD and disability, but realistically, these could be relevant for anybody within a workplace who needs support to do their job for reasons outside of their control. With a workplace culture based on trust and flexibility, changes could be made easily and upon request.

However, this is not the case for many workplaces, who may either under or over react to a request such as this, with significant potential for misunderstanding - especially if the people involved haven't received training on accommodating disabilities at work.

In the case of an under-reaction, a request for support may simply be ignored, or vague assurances may be provided but not followed up. From my experiences of working with employers, challenges arise when a request is misunderstood or treated as another 'task' on a list, such as being forwarded on to HR, with no clear reassurance, interim support, or timeframes communicated to the employee.

Asking for help is a deeply vulnerable thing to do for an employee, and the immediate response will be extremely important in helping to ease or increase their anxiety levels. Having a compassionate and empathetic reaction makes sense, providing reassurance, and offering supportive measures in the interim until it's understood by everybody what the next steps will look like. A request like this should be treated seriously, but compassionately.

In contrast, an over-reaction might include hasty discussions being had out of fear and anxiety on the side of the employer about what to do next. An individual should obviously never be treated badly for asking for a reasonable adjustment, as this would constitute to an act of victimisation, but receiving a formal and cold response from HR, possibly inviting them to a meeting without any context, or arranging an Occupational Health assessment on their behalf, for example, can feel incredibly stressful.

The individual may very likely be nervous about talking to HR, and scared about their future career progression, including potentially being told they can't do their job at all. Providing reassurance throughout is extremely important, and emphasising the importance and benefits of them having asked for help.

Finally, these types of requests may be misunderstood, and put through inappropriate channels.

A common example is a request to work at home as a reasonable adjustment, which an employer may consider under a Flexible Working Policy, for example, instead of one related to disability.

It's important to note that adjustments are not made only in response to 'problems' that are clear to everybody - there doesn't need to be 'proof', or a 'reason' for this. People who are struggling, and those who are brave enough to ask for help with these struggles, should be believed and supported at work.

Reasonable adjustments being denied

Although the Equality Act places a legal duty on employers to make reasonable adjustments for people with disabilities at work, the confusion in applying this law may easily result in it being applied incorrectly. Failure to make reasonable adjustments can amount to discrimination under the Equality Act, so this is potentially a very serious and expensive mistake to make for an employer.

There's many different reasons behind adjustments being denied. A common scenario involves requests for adjustments at interview, where these are simply denied outright. For an employer, this may feel more straightforward, as interviews are largely standardised processes, as opposed to the ongoing management of a human being in their day to day life at work. Also, the applicant is unlikely to know how to take this denial much further!

I have supported people who have been denied adjustments at this stage, which from my perspective, could have easily amounted to discrimination under the Equality Act. These requests were usually very easy to implement, such as providing the interview questions in advance.

I've also supported employers who have been very anxious and uncertain about how to implement these kinds of requests. In an event I held for HR professionals, one asked me, 'at what point would it be fair to share the interview questions, to ensure it doesn't disadvantage the other interviewees?'

The answer is simple: it doesn't matter about everyone else. Requests for reasonable adjustments should all be considered in line with a series of standard considerations, such as those outlined in chapter 'Reasonable Adjustments for ADHD'. Each one should be considered uniquely - just because something works for one person, doesn't mean it works for everybody. If you're so worried about managing the expectations of non-disabled people, just offer them the same support. Adjustments are about supporting the individual who needs it - not other people.

We did this recently with an interview for in house coaches at ADHD Works. Some applicants requested the interview questions in advance, which made me realise how much better it would be for everybody, including ourselves, if everyone had the option to access these questions. By telling them what we were expecting, we could judge them on how well they can prepare, not panic!

This type of anxiety is also seen in the workplace, post-recruitment. Most reasons I have heard for an employer failing to make a reasonable adjustment is that 'it wouldn't be fair to everybody else'. One even said that if they helped that individual, they would have to help other people in the same situations, which is exactly the point of the law.

Often, adjustments are simply not implemented because the expectation is on the individual to follow this up, which can be extremely demoralising and humiliating to do. For example, if someone has an Occupational Health assessment with recommendations made to their employer, the duty should *not* be on the individual to arrange a follow up conversation about how these will be implemented.

To resolve these types of situations, it's important to have a clear policy in place outlining the processes to be followed in determining how a decision can be made about implementing a reasonable adjustment, as in chapter 'Disability vs Diversity'. Training is then required to ensure everybody understands and follows this!

Individuals could then be signposted towards this policy during the process, which can help provide a structure for decisions being made. If it is not reasonable to make a certain adjustment, reasons should be provided (that aren't discriminatory!) and alternatives should be discussed.

As in chapter 'Reasonable Adjustments for ADHD', it's important to remember that when requesting adjustments, employers only have a duty to implement them if they are 'reasonable', and so it's important to strike a balance when making specific requests. For example, requesting software to support your role which costs an employer £20,000 may not be deemed reasonable, whereas another solution that costs £2000 might be. What is deemed reasonable will vary based on the size of the employer, resources available to it, and alternative solutions it has in place.

If you are an individual experiencing these challenges, although it may feel extremely difficult to advocate for yourself, you may have to do so in order to access this support. Following up on requests for reasonable adjustments does not make you a burden, or 'difficult' - it's a good thing for your employer to support you to do your job in the best way possible!

If you have been refused reasonable adjustments because of a reason you think is incorrect, such as because it wouldn't be fair to other people, you can discuss your options with a trade union representative or lawyer.

Talking about ADHD in other contexts

Everyone who is diagnosed with ADHD will have their own unique experiences of this. For many people, it may bring them a lot of relief, understanding, and validation. They may wish to share this with other people, helping them to access the support that may have taken them a very long time to reach.

Employers may not know how to respond to this. For example, one employment tribunal case relating to disability discrimination involved an employee who said she was told that she talked about ADHD too much on social media, for example (the employee won!).[25]

The lines between work and social media can be blurry for everybody, but employers should consider extremely carefully any opinions they may have about what any employee of theirs chooses to do outside of working hours - especially when this relates to their health condition!

Within an organisation itself, an employee with ADHD may wish to talk about their ADHD to others, such as within teams or an Employee Resource Group. This can be extremely helpful in raising awareness and providing opportunities for passionate employees to support others.

---

25 https://www.gov.uk/employment-tribunal-decisions/ms-p-singh-v-manhattan-partners-ltd-2404707-slash-2022, https://www.youtube.com/watch?v=duaLbfR2qYk

I have worked with various employees who have been asked to do organisation wide training and talks about their experiences, in addition to chairing meetings and networks, so it's equally important to ensure that these types of requests are very carefully handled.

Although a person might feel motivated to share their experiences at first, the nature of ADHD means they may not have thought through all of the potential consequences of doing so, including their workload, and later wish to change their minds! I also strongly advise reflecting this additional work appropriately. Although it might not feel like work, it is!

Colleagues talking about ADHD in other contexts

Some employees may also talk about ADHD in a variety of contexts that may be less than helpful. As it has become more popular in the news, it feels like a stigmatising narrative has emerged around 'everybody having ADHD'.[26] These kinds of conversations, particularly when they are being featured by national media outlets can be incredibly damaging and harmful on an individual level.

ADHD is obviously a very real and valid medical condition, with the same regulation and oversight as

26 https://www.dailymail.co.uk/femail/article-11715691/DR-MAX-PEMBERTON-According-test-Ive-got-ADHD-Ludicrous.html

other medical conditions, if not more. Nevertheless, people with ADHD should never be expected to prove that their ADHD is 'real', especially in a workplace context. Harmful discussions like this happening in the workplace can be extremely damaging and potentially result in legal considerations for an employer in relation to providing a safe working environment. The Equality Act places a duty on employers to ensure that disabled people are protected from discrimination at work, regardless of individual disclosure.

If a person has disclosed ADHD at work, it's obviously important that they are not discriminated against because of this. It might feel unclear if they choose to discuss this with their colleagues as to how others should respond, but training can help with this. There should not be any discriminatory comments made towards an individual, such as, for example, 'you don't really have ADHD'.

Employers can contribute to overall knowledge and education by providing training, as in chapter 'Creating an ADHD Friendly Culture'. They can also make clear in policies and communications that discrimination, harassment and bullying of any kind is not tolerated, and provide clear routes to de-escalate any conflict that arises of this nature.

Bullying, Harassment and Victimisation

There's no law against bullying in the UK, unless you are bullied because of or in relation to a protected characteristic such as disability, in which case it could constitute harassment. This means behaviour that creates a hostile or intimidating environment, or violates a person's dignity.

Essentially, environments must not be created or tolerated at work where a disabled person may be subject to unwanted, offensive, or exploitative behaviour in relation to their disability.

There are different levels of this. For example, actively making comments about ADHD towards a person, such as saying, 'your ADHD must be bad today, you can't shut up', could constitute harassment.

Alternatively, a person may feel harassed as a result of their ADHD in relation to how they have been treated because of this, which may not be explicit. For example, they may feel harassed by being shut down whenever they speak in meetings. Victimisation may occur when a person is treated differently because of a protected act, such as raising a grievance about disability discrimination.

An employee represents the employer in terms of its actions or behaviour. This means that, in most cases, the actions of an individual employee at work are considered an action of the employer, regardless of whether an employer had knowledge or gave consent for such action. To defend this, an employer must be able to show that they took all reasonable steps to prevent the individual from discriminating, which again emphasises the importance of having disability training and policies in place.

An employee is personally responsible for their own acts of discrimination, harassment or victimisation, even if they were unaware that their actions were against the law. This is only excused if they were told there was nothing wrong with their behaviour, and they reasonably believed this to be true.

Essentially, employers must ensure that everybody in an organisation understands the importance of behaving with respect towards each other, and have anti-bullying policies in place. Specifically in relation to disability, it's extremely important to ensure that all employees understand that they must not discriminate, harass, or victimise other employees, and the legal duty for an employer to make reasonable adjustments as under the Equality Act. Having induction training on these subjects is strongly advisable!

If you are an individual experiencing bullying, harassment, victimisation or any other kinds of discrimination, I'm really sorry - I know this must be incredibly stressful. Again, I'd strongly recommend talking to your trade union representative or a lawyer who can help you to understand your options: this should not be happening.

Feedback and communication issues

As people with ADHD may experience challenges with emotional regulation and Rejection Sensitive Dysphoria, it's important to take extra care around feedback and communications. As in 'Reasonable Adjustments for ADHD', this can be as simple as mindfully providing positive feedback.

If this management style does not come naturally to a person, they may understandably struggle with this. For example, one manager I knew said they preferred not to provide excessively positive feedback in case the person stopped trying. As in 'Managing ADHD for Success', this is the opposite of how a person with ADHD will thrive at work!

Challenges may arise during 'official' feedback periods, such as during an annual review. This can also be difficult to navigate in terms of future career progression and learning opportunities. For example, many people with ADHD I know have lots of wonderful ideas for the workplace that may not fit into a corporate box, and they can feel very disillusioned if these are outright rejected at work.

Communication challenges may also arise in relation to engaging with others, such as if an employee struggles with particular relationships or areas of work. For example, they may find it difficult to say no to requests from colleagues to take on additional work, or to update them about their own timeframes and ability to meet deadlines.

These kinds of issues can be swiftly supported with regular check ins from a manager or mentor, helping an individual to feel safe enough to raise any concerns or challenges they have in a judgement free space. It's important that regular positive reassurance is provided, and the context of negative feedback is provided in detail. People with ADHD may be very eager to improve, but it can feel very demoralising if the path to do so isn't clearly set out.

If you are an employee with ADHD, remember that you deserve support, and these challenges are not your fault. Having coaching or therapy can be very helpful to tackle these challenges, such as by creating time buffers between saying 'yes' to new work, and regularly reviewing your calendar and workload. You don't have to do it all, and your 50% effort level at work is likely to be other people's 150%!

Performance issues

ADHD may become relevant in the workplace in relation to performance issues. There are many different scenarios where this could happen, from probation, in setting clear expectations that a person can reasonably meet, to periods where symptoms may worsen, for example.

I've worked with many employers who have only found out about a person having ADHD after these issues have been raised with them. It's important for them to take this disclosure seriously and provide the necessary adjustments to support an individual to do their job as their colleagues are able to.

Again, a person is under no duty to disclose a disability to their employer, but by creating inclusive cultures, this can hopefully happen earlier where performance issues do not happen.

ADHD symptoms may manifest differently at different times for a person, often becoming much worse with stress. This is because of our impacted executive functioning skills, which means that if we are struggling to regulate our emotions, for example, this might impact our ability to 'do what we know' in other areas as well, such as meeting our day to day expectations at work.

Being put on a Performance Improvement Plan should obviously not be a response to someone telling their employer they have ADHD! If ADHD emerges at the same time as discussions about such a plan, it's important to consider the impact of these symptoms on performance, and to ensure that these are treated separately. Having ADHD is not a performance issue!

Appropriate conversations should take place about support and adjustments, and the expectations around performance should be explicitly clear, including the steps a person can take to meet these, particularly in light of their disability. It may be helpful to involve a third party at this point, such as an Occupational Health expert, who can provide expert recommendations of how to improve overall performance and wellbeing at work.

Absences and long-term sickness

ADHD is not an illness in itself, and doesn't fit neatly into a box when describing a reason for absence. For example, having ADHD most likely results in me experiencing migraines, overwhelm, burnout, and anxiety, which might prevent me from working. I've also had a variety of challenges that have arisen directly from having ADHD which impacted my ability to work, from a hot water bottle exploding in my face after trying to make it in under 2 minutes and forgetting to read the instructions, to accidentally taking too many ADHD medication tablets in the morning.

It's not like the flu, or food poisoning. The majority of challenges I experience at work are due to my ADHD, and sometimes I need a reset day. However, this can be very difficult to apply in a formal working environment, where there are often policies in place, monitoring how long a person is able to be off work due to sickness.

These policies can be nonsensical for the average person, such as only allowing them a certain number of sickness periods in a year before triggering a review process. We obviously can't control when we get sick, but anxiety around not being able to take any sick days within a certain period may feel very stressful, especially if we have ADHD.

Employers should make clear to employees that adjustments can be made to these policies in case of a disability such as ADHD for example. It's also important to provide reassurance, so individuals understand that taking time off work because of their disability does not contribute to them not being able to do their job.

If a person is off sick for a long period of time, or is simply unable to do their job because of their ADHD, this may require a formal decision about their future ability to return to work. Employers can talk to HR advisers and lawyers about the best course of action to take, which will be highly dependent on the situation.

If you're an employee in this situation, you can talk to your employer about the best course of action in supporting you to return to work when you feel well enough to do so.

Complaints, Grievances and Formal Questions

If an employee is experiencing challenges at work because of their ADHD, they may make a formal complaint. The procedure for this should be set out in an accessible policy, such as a Grievance Procedure, facilitating informal conflict resolution as a first step. As employees may feel uncomfortable complaining to their line manager, for example, providing alternative or anonymous routes of communication to HR can be extremely useful.

This complaint can also escalate into or emerge as a Grievance, which is a formal complaint to an employer, usually triggering an investigation and decision. This is not a decision to take lightly, and may be extremely stressful to experience. By nature, it is an adversarial process, turning nuanced issues into a 'right or wrong' situation.

For someone with ADHD, this process can trigger intense anxiety and rumination. Whilst this is one of many issues for an employer to manage, for an employee, their entire career and future may be at stake. It's very important that individuals can access mental health support during this time, either through an Employee Assistance Programme, or privately. This could also mean they are not well enough to work during the grievance process and be signed off sick as a result.

It's important to seek advice before making a decision like this, as it can have very significant consequences. For example, if you're considering making a formal complaint, you can talk to your trade union, Citizens Advice, or a lawyer before doing so, thinking about the realistic possible outcomes and what you'd like from your future.

Having a clear timeline of issues and written evidence is very important when making a Grievance, along with identifying what you would like to happen next. The Equality Act 2010 also enables a 'Formal Questions Procedure' which is a formal procedure allowing a person to ask their employer questions about discrimination relating to their situation. An employer must usually answer these questions otherwise 'adverse inferences' may be drawn about them if the situation goes before a tribunal.

For example, asking a question about why a reasonable adjustment was not implemented can be very helpful to understand whether the law was correctly followed. These questions should be submitted in writing as a 'questionnaire', and it should be made clear that the questions require action to be taken by an employer.[27]

There may be situations where 'off the record' conversations can happen about the future of an employee in light of challenges that have arisen, which cannot be disclosed in future legal proceedings.

If there is no formal dispute, an employer may ask an employee for a 'protected conversation', where they may offer a payment in return for terminating a contract with an individual. This cannot be used

---

27 https://workingfamilies.org.uk/articles/the-questionnaire-the-equality-act-2010-discrimination-and-other-prohibited-conduct-questions-and-answers-forms/

to discriminate against someone. I have heard of this happening to a person after they requested reasonable adjustments to be made, which obviously resulted in a claim of disability discrimination!

A 'without prejudice' negotiation can occur when there is already a dispute in place or a formal dispute is envisaged, such as a Grievance. Such a conversation must be expressly marked as 'without prejudice' and the discussion must be a genuine attempt to resolve the dispute, off the record. I'd strongly suggest seeking the advice of a trade union representative or lawyer if you end up in this situation, who will be able to help de-escalate it.

It's important to remember that a person with ADHD can still request reasonable adjustments throughout these processes. As an employer, making these processes simple and objective is important to be able to de-escalate conflict as efficiently as possible.

Enlisting the services of a mediator, especially one skilled in supporting neurodivergent people, may be a very wise decision to make early on to avoid needlessly stressful situations for everybody.

Employment tribunals

If the situation is not resolved from a Grievance, this may escalate into a claim that is held before an employment tribunal. Whilst employment tribunal awards are uncapped in cases of disability discrimination and a person is not required to have a certain length of employment, or to pay anything to take their employer to a tribunal, reaching this point is likely to be very difficult in reality.

Firstly, all internal processes, such as Grievance procedures (including appeals) must be exhausted before a tribunal claim can be brought. Certain time limits must also be met for a claim to be brought, usually 3 months minus 1 day from when an event happened. However, it should be noted that the time limit freezes during the period of 'Early Acas Conciliation' with Acas, as outlined below.

This can be confusing to figure out, especially if a person is complaining about something *not* happening, such as a failure to make reasonable adjustments (which would be the date the decision was made not to offer the reasonable adjustment to a person).

Going through grievance, disciplinary or appeal procedures does not change this time limit. A legal expert should be able to help with identifying this, but that's why it's a good idea for a person to understand their rights and relevant timeframes prior to making any formal complaints.

An individual will also need to inform an organisation called Acas about their application to a tribunal, and then participate in 'Early Acas Conciliation', which are essentially free mediation services aimed at resolving the issue. If unsuccessful, the claim will progress to a tribunal stage, where it's possible that an individual will need to engage the services of a solicitor. Legal fees can be extremely expensive, and an employer will very likely have legal representation.

It can take a very long time for a person to receive a hearing date for an employment tribunal case - on average, from 6 months to 1 year. It can take 2-3 years from the point of issuing a claim to reaching a final hearing.[28]

Settlements can be agreed prior to a tribunal hearing date, as it rarely makes commercial sense to go ahead with an employment tribunal claim. However, the person complaining may feel very strongly and on a point of principle, want to go ahead, and I have worked with many people who have ADHD who are motivated by the strong sense of social justice and fairness in wanting to make things better for others.

If this resonates with you, please put yourself first and get out of this situation as quickly as you can. It can be extremely stressful and cast a shadow over your entire life until the hearing, and even if you get the result you're looking for, you will still have lost a huge chunk of your life in battling this fight. You cannot control the actions of anybody else, especially employers (and especially after you've left!), and

---

28 https://www.frettens.co.uk/site/blog/employment-blog/waiting-times-employment-tribunal-hearings-increase-backlog

it's very unlikely that you will end up back in your old role after going through a process like this.

You may be awarded financial compensation, but this is dependent on a number of factors, including your ability to prove financial loss (meaning that you might not be able to work for a long period of time!).

ADHD challenges at work can be extremely stressful to navigate, but they can also be extremely easy to resolve. This requires human to human compassion, clarity, collaboration and compromise.

Although these issues may feel as though the world is ending, it's important to remember that the issues will come to an end, and on an individual level, it's better to work in a place where you can be yourself, and be happy! If it is revenge that you instinctively desire, then the best revenge is to move on with a life well lived.

For employers, it's in your interest to resolve these issues and prevent them from happening in the first place. As we will see in the following chapters, people with ADHD are huge assets to any workplace, and it's a huge shame to lose somebody as a result of challenges that could be so easily resolved.

Harnessing ADHD

Chapter 8
ADHD Strengths

It's common to hear ADHD be referred to as a 'superpower'. As in chapter 'Spotting ADHD at Work', there are certain benefits and challenges that come with having ADHD, but these do not exist in isolation.

There are incredible strengths and unique abilities associated with ADHD, but these can also be very challenging and difficult to live with. For example, my ability to hyper-focus and interest-based nervous system have helped me to publish 3 books successfully, but I also struggle significantly with workaholism and relaxing. This has a debilitating impact on my life and health overall, as I feel much more comfortable working than not!

The 'superpower' narrative of ADHD is also commonly linked to productivity and capitalism. It doesn't help that the medication most often associated with ADHD is stimulants, evoking images of university students taking pills to stay awake and study all night for their exams. As 'pills don't give skills', this is largely unfounded - I've coached students who have been unable to do anything but rewrite a certain paragraph repeatedly because of their medication. It can help us to focus, but doesn't necessarily help us to choose *on what.* ADHD is ultimately a challenge with regulating our attention, as opposed to a 'deficit' of it.

Nevertheless, there *are* many strengths associated with ADHD (in my opinion, anyway!). A 2018 study found that hardly any empirical research had been done about the positive aspects of ADHD previously, with previous content mainly focusing on results about treatment, as opposed to the inherent benefits of having ADHD.[29]

Here's a few of the benefits of having ADHD, and how these can show up at work:

1) Innovation and creativity

Having ADHD means that we *literally* think differently to 'most' people. Growing up in a neurotypical world with a neurodivergent brain means that we've likely developed 'creative adjustments' to the things we struggle to do 'normally'.

If we all thought in exactly the same way, there would be much less innovation and creativity in the world. Take the example of David Beckham, a footballer who's well known for his exceptional abilities. If an

---

29 https://pubmed.ncbi.nlm.nih.gov/30374709/ (Sedgwick et al., 2018)

entire team was made up of David Beckham clones, there would simply be lots of people who are excellent at the same things, but it is the integration of a broad variety of different skills in a team that is crucial in order to achieve the team's success.

The same goes for workplaces - and life in general. We are living at a time with extreme uncertainty and disruption, and we need people who can think fast and outside of the box. Problems can't be solved with the same thinking that created them. At its core, this means doing things differently, which is incredibly valuable in a world where standing out is crucial to success.

At work, this could show up in anything from simply the ways we do our jobs, with the unique flair and innovation that makes our working styles different to 'most' people, to providing feedback and ideas in the ways that we solve problems. For example, at ADHD Works, we provide interview questions to interviewees in advance - this is hardly a groundbreaking idea, but it certainly felt that way when we heard the positive feedback as a result!

2) Hyper-focus, energy and an interest-based nervous system

The ability to do a huge amount of work in a very short period of time can be exceptionally useful, especially when managed and supported effectively so we can avoid burnout. In my job, I could do a month's worth of work in a few days. This being said, some tasks that took others 5 minutes would take me 5 hours, such as filling in excel sheets, so providing support for this would enable me to be as highly productive as possible at work by staying in my 'zone of genius'.

Research has found that adults with ADHD have had more real-time creative achievements than those without, demonstrating the power of our innate creativity and ability to work 'in flow'.[30]

Once we understand how our interest based nervous system works, we can hack it to regulate our focus. I like to think of this as surfing waves - when I feel the wave of hyper-focus coming, I jump on the wave to surf it, knowing to build in rest and breaks in advance.

As people with ADHD typically need *more* stimulation rather than less, this means that we have exceptionally high value within the workplace. Tasks that are challenging and have a sense of urgency or pressure associated with them, such as presenting in court or saving lives as an emergency responder, may feel very easy for us in comparison to others who do not thrive on this stimulation. As our work becomes more reliant on technology to do tasks that can be easily automated, the importance of these skills will become ever more apparent.

---

30 https://totallyadd.com/wp-content/uploads/White_Shah_ ADHDCreativity_PAID.pdf

3) Authenticity and honesty

Having ADHD means I often have no choice but to be entirely myself. If I mask my symptoms or who I am, this feels like lying, seriously impacting my energy levels and motivation. On the contrary, embracing and accepting myself has seen me thrive in my career, doing talks for well-known international companies.

I felt extremely scared about these beforehand, but realised that all I need to do is show up and be authentically me - which makes it very easy! Neurotypical people are said to have the ability to 'think before speaking', but I am often finding out what I'm thinking at the same time as everybody else, as a verbal processor. This means I am utterly incapable of lying - which is a good thing!

In the workplace, having people show up entirely as themselves saves a considerable amount of energy in masking, and being honest and direct is beneficial for everybody. Honesty and clear communication in the workplace is vitally important for any issues to be solved promptly and effectively. Empowering people to be themselves at work is what leads to the best results for organisations, providing the space for creativity, mistakes, learning and growth to thrive in the long run.

4) Enthusiasm, loyalty and passion

In my experience, people with ADHD tend to be extremely engaged in workplaces where they feel accepted and supported as themselves. Our interest based nervous system means that we can be incredibly enthusiastic about the work we do. Whenever I've had jobs where I've felt supported and aligned with my work, I have dedicated myself 150%.

This could be to our detriment, if we don't have frameworks in place to receive our enthusiasm, such as by having workplaces receptive to our ideas and feedback, but can be easily managed with systems such as 'ideas days'. It could also feel frustrating if our colleagues aren't as passionate as we are about the work, but having ways to connect with this ourselves and feel fulfilled is important. For example, by becoming involved with like-minded peers and joining an Employee Resource Group or society.

In general, the loyalty, passion and enthusiasm that can come from supporting an ADHD employee can be extremely valuable within a workplace. Engaged employees also inspire others to be motivated and proud of their workplace.

For example, when I started talking about ADHD at work, I was contacted by someone who wanted to share how brilliant her manager and employer had been in supporting her at work. We went on to record a LinkedIn live event with not only the individual, but also her manager, showcasing their best practice not only internally, but also externally to potential clients. Happy employees will result in a happy culture, leading to results for everybody.

5) Bravery and curiosity

The bravery aspect of ADHD can be linked with our tendency for impulsivity. Although we might 'act before thinking' from time to time, this can also mean that our brilliant ideas become reality. This is the secret behind ADHD Works - I've often started ideas like ADHD retreats before I've had time to think them through properly!

Curiosity has been strongly linked to ADHD, in addition to being open to new experiences and having a desire to learn.[31] As a result, ADHD employees tend to have a growth mindset, embracing challenges and discomfort in the pursuit of learning and development. This makes us excellent employees who can adapt and adjust along with our work as needed.

Empowering people to work in the ways that work best for them, such as with flexible working hours or locations, ultimately means we trust them to try out ideas and risk failure. Personally, I believe my ADHD tendency for bravery, risk-taking and comfort with mistakes makes me good at my job. I know that perfection doesn't exist, and success is on the other side of fear.

---

31   https://link.springer.com/article/10.1007/s12402-018-0277-6 (Zuss 2012)

For employers, this means trusting employees who don't fit into a traditional 'professional' box, and providing psychological safety for people to get it wrong and make mistakes. For example, embracing and believing people who have 'squiggly' career histories and many different jobs, instead of interrogating gaps! Prioritise honesty and authenticity over people who remain in positions where they're unhappy just 'for their CV' - our past doesn't define our present.

6) Compassion and a strong sense of social justice

People with ADHD tend to be extraordinarily compassionate towards others, possibly due to experiencing a strong range of emotions ourselves. Experiencing Rejection Sensitive Dysphoria may motivate us to help others to avoid feeling these intense feelings of shame, and having been through many challenges ourselves, it can be fulfilling to use these to help others avoid similar experiences.

Having ADHD can be very lonely at times, but understanding this about ourselves can be an amazing way to instantly connect with others. In the groups of people with ADHD I have coached, they all connect on a deeper level than making small talk, feeling seen, heard and validated by others who think like them.

Suffering from rejection throughout our lives because of being different can mean that we are hyper-sensitive to including and supporting others around us. For example, having been bullied myself as a child, I would always stand up for someone being treated in this way as an adult. This can be very important for workplaces, where bullying or poor treatment can be pervasive and hidden behind closed doors.

Having people who are willing to stand up for what they believe in is extremely important, especially when these beliefs are aligned to the values of a company, such as inclusion. This also makes us very caring and supportive colleagues, forming important parts of teams and excellent managers. If we can manage ourselves, others are easy! ADHD has been scientifically linked to optimism, persuasiveness, and an energy that vitalises and inspires others around them - which are rare and brilliant qualities to have in employees.[32]

7) Resilience and tenacity

Living with ADHD can be extremely challenging at times, but it makes us survivors. Having a brain that is constantly blaring 150 channels at you can be exhausting, but it makes us resilient. The hundreds

---

32   https://pubmed.ncbi.nlm.nih.gov/30374709/ (Sedgwick et al. 2018)

of people I have met with ADHD are all extremely tenacious, strong, and resilient people.

Daring to embrace our differences in a world where we're expected to fit in comes with rewards. When I quit my secure job in law to become an ADHD Coach, I wasn't worried, because I know how hard of a worker I am. I could get a job in a shop, restaurant, as a yoga teacher, model, caterer - anything - and I would make it work. As it happens, because ADHD coaching was such a bizarre and relatively new career at the time, I was inundated with clients immediately, because most people stayed in their 'normal' jobs. My partner at the time pleaded with me to line up a 'safe' 9-5 job alongside coaching until I was secure, but I knew this would distract me from my goal - and I was right. The safest option for me was going all in, working hard, and trusting myself.

People with ADHD tend to be similarly tenacious. We've likely struggled with immense challenges throughout our lives, such as trauma - including that of actually accessing a diagnosis![33]

Translated to our work, this can see us achieve incredible feats, because we're used to putting in effort. In my experience, people with ADHD put a huge amount of effort into everything they do, and don't give up easily.

---

33 https://www.ncbi.nlm.nih.gov/pmc/articles/PMC5973996/

How to harness these strengths

ADHD is defined when our symptoms reach a certain level of 'Disorder', but things don't have to stay that way. Once we understand how our brain works, we can work *with* it, instead of against it. As an ADHD Coach, I have seen countless people completely transform as a result of accepting themselves and their unique working styles instead of trying to force themselves into a box they were never going to fit into.

On an individual basis, people can harness their ADHD at work by understanding what their unique strengths and challenges are and how they show up. Identifying the support that can help us, and actually asking for this, is crucially important to enable us to reach our full potential in harnessing these skills.

Then, we can look at how much we are using our unique strengths on a day to day basis. If there are areas this could be improved, we could take the initiative to try and increase how we use our strengths, particularly at work. When we do the things we're already good at, our confidence grows.

I often hear about people wanting to 'reach their full potential', as though this is at the top of a mountain they can and must climb. Realistically, our 'full potential' is constantly shifting. Learning how to work with our strengths and access support for our challenges, instead of beating ourselves up for them, is an excellent and highly achievable middle ground.

Once we're able to exist in this place, with the full knowledge and acceptance that some days will be better than others, we can do exceptional things and live a happier life, overall.

For some people, this might include things like writing books or doing speeches, whereas for others (including myself), it might look like staying in the same job for a certain period of time. We get to define what 'harnessing our strengths' means to us, but for me, this ultimately comes down to self-compassion.

On the contrary, employers can harness ADHD at work by simply providing the right environment for it to thrive, and for this self-compassion to happen. Just recruiting people with ADHD won't necessarily achieve much without the right culture and support in place for them to form part of a diverse, psychologically healthy team. Equipping people with appropriate training, knowledge, and skills, such as ADHD coaching skills, enables them to create these environments.

If we imagine a plant failing to thrive, this looks like equipping people with the knowledge of how to help that plant thrive again. This also looks like providing them with the space and flexibility to make changes as needed, such as trying out different locations, and creativity and trust to collaborate on ideas, such as adding more or less soil or fertiliser. Human beings are essentially the same.

Now, if we imagine this plant is different from the typical kind of plants a person may be used to looking after, such as an orchid, it's reasonable to assume that that person will need specific training to know how to avoid killing it! What works for most plants won't necessarily work for the orchid, so they may need additional support in understanding what can help that orchid to thrive.

Harnessing ADHD at work is largely similar to this. With the right support in place, the results can be incredible.

To harness our strengths, we need to firstly understand what they are. The ADHD Strengths quiz in this chapter can help a person with ADHD identify what their strengths are and how much they're using them in their day to day life. The free online 'VIA Character' traits test may help inform this![34]

---

34 https://www.viacharacter.org

ADHD & Strengths
Quiz

This quiz can help someone understand how to identify & harness their ADHD strengths in their day to day life.

QUESTIONS	RATING SCALE				
	Never	Rarely	Sometimes	Often	Always
Out-of-the-box thinking e.g having lots of ideas & unique problem-solving	○	○	○	○	○
Hyper-focus e.g feeling 'in flow' when doing something of interest	○	○	○	○	○
Bravery e.g going ahead with your new ideas or standing up for our beliefs	○	○	○	○	○
Creativity e.g connecting dots others can't & being original!	○	○	○	○	○
Compassion e.g kindness & care towards others	○	○	○	○	○
Enthusiasm e.g feeling very passionate, with a strong sense of justice	○	○	○	○	○
Energy e.g having a lot of physical or mental energy to use up!	○	○	○	○	○
Resilience e.g being very good at failing, learning & trying again!	○	○	○	○	○

Tip: use the 'VIA character strengths' quiz!

Chapter 9
ADHD Coaching Skills

To harness ADHD at work, employees can be trained in ADHD coaching skills. This is quite a specific niche, but given that there's been a 400% increase in adults seeking assessments since 2020 (and you're reading this book!) - it's obviously highly in demand.[35]

I trained as an ADHD coach with US based organisation ADDCA, choosing to invest in this instead of qualifying as a solicitor. Since the second I started working as a coach, the demand for ADHD coaching has been so high that I've created courses, corporate trainings, and even an ADHD Works training and certification programme for other ADHD coaches. This is due to people desperately in need of support, including the reason for this book.

ADHD coaching is very different from 'normal' coaching, because it accounts for the unique qualities of ADHD that can influence how we access and engage with support. When I was diagnosed with

---

35 https://www.theguardian.com/society/2023/jan/13/adhd-services-swamped-say-experts-as-more-uk-women-seek-diagnosis

ADHD, I'd tried everything from therapy to energy coaching, desperate to find something that didn't tell me what I already knew, that made me feel shame for not being able to engage in it properly.

This all changed when I had ADHD coaching for the first time. Talking to someone who validated my experiences and understood how my brain worked gave me hope that I could overcome the challenges that had made the first 25 years of my life so difficult that I couldn't cope.

Coaching is all about moving forwards, and ADHD coaching accounts for the fact that people with ADHD struggle to 'do what they know'. It's a collaborative process, designed to accommodate for our unique ways of thinking and provide support to help us understand our brains and work with them, instead of against them.

In the workplace, these skills can be extremely useful - not just for colleagues of employees with ADHD, but everyone living in our attention-economy world. This is why I created the ADHD Champions course, training employees to support each other with these skills.

Here's an overview of what they are and how to use them to harness ADHD at work:

1) Active Listening

Our society places huge importance on public speaking, but not so much on listening. Being able to truly listen to another person and enable them to feel seen and heard is a highly underrated skill. This is even more important with a person who has ADHD, as we can often verbally process our thoughts as we're thinking them and second guessing what we're saying, especially given how the executive functioning skill of self-awareness is affected by ADHD.

Having somebody who can literally and metaphorically keep up with us and our whizzy thoughts (and words!) can be extremely powerful. From the perspective of a coach, actively listening essentially involves ensuring the person we're talking to knows that we are listening to them, focusing on what they're saying instead of what we want to say next. Instead of bringing the conversation back around to us or jumping in with advice, we can instead simply summarise what we've heard and check that we've understood properly.

This can be very helpful for a person with ADHD to reflect on and process their own words, in addition to feeling validated and heard without judgement. This is especially important in a workplace context, where we may be feeling on edge or anxious, such as when talking to people who are senior to us. The key part of active listening is not to impart any judgement, but simply to hear a person as they are.

The skill of active listening is one of the most powerful I have as an entrepreneur, in addition to being an ADHD Coach. I've used it in meetings with some of the world's biggest organisations, such as with Directors of the World Health Organization, where I was able to listen and respond appropriately instead of saying what *I* wanted to hear. Truly listening to people is a real gift, and taking the time to learn how to break this down, such as by repeating back a person's words to them and saying things like, 'what I'm hearing is..', or 'it sounds like...' is extremely effective.

2) Setting the 'agenda'

We don't typically think about the structure of a conversation, but coaching conversations generally have a framework whereby a person is able to move forward as a result. In 'neurotypical' styles of coaching, the person being coached is usually expected to provide the agenda for the conversation, explaining what they would like to walk away with at the outset and providing a framework for the conversation.

Coaching through an ADHD lens means that we understand the difficulties a person with ADHD may have with this due to their impacted self-awareness. I experienced this myself in coaching, once driven to tears from a person who refused to do anything until I told her what I 'wanted' to do as the client, but this kind of pressure made me freeze up in overwhelm.

So as an ADHD coach myself, I am always providing reassurance to the person I'm talking to that they don't have to know what they want to get out of the conversation. Taking the pressure off and having ADHD knowledge myself as a foundation, such as being able to walk through the executive functioning impacts of ADHD, always seems to be very helpful for people with ADHD.

In a workplace context, you can provide reassurance and examples of conversations or scripts (such as those at the end of this chapter) to people with ADHD who may be looking to have a conversation about it. They may not know exactly what kind of support they need, but just know they need something! Being diagnosed with ADHD can be an overwhelming experience which leaves us wondering 'what now?' - especially if someone has been on a waiting list for assessment for years!

For coaching, this agenda is important because it provides the container for the conversation where the coach is essentially holding the space and focusing on the person being coached, helping them to move towards that outcome. Collaboratively setting or agreeing the purpose of the conversation at the beginning can be very helpful to move a person forward.

3) Filtering

Once the agenda for a conversation is set, a coach can filter the conversation to maintain consistency and grounding, supporting the person they are coaching to move forward and avoid going off on tangents (in a shame-free way!). Due to the differences in how we think and communicate, people with ADHD may become distracted by their own thoughts, distracting us in the process from the purpose of the conversation.

This is why I believe that if you can coach a person with ADHD, you can coach anybody! I am often having to gently ground and interrupt the people I coach as they try to tell me very interesting stories about their lives or ask me questions about my own! In my experience, we can talk quite quickly, and share lots of information that may not necessarily be connected in one go. This means that as a coach, we need to be actively listening and focused to be able to filter through what is and is not relevant to the conversation.

It's important to do this in a non-judgmental way, which can look like setting expectations at the start of the session and asking permission to interrupt if the conversation goes off track. When doing this, I always comment on how interesting it is (because it is!), but I remind them of the time remaining and ask how they would like to spend it. Alternatively I might simply validate what has been said and direct the conversation back to the agenda.

As coaches, we're listening to what is and isn't being said. I can usually filter through a conversation to understand the 'real' reason behind the way a person is feeling, such as by noticing things they quickly rush in at the end. Picking up on changes in language and tone are important to help us catch what's going on behind the many thoughts and words coming at us.

4) Curious Questions

Coaching is essentially all about asking the right questions, which can help guide a person to their own expertise. As 99% of advice given isn't taken, and what works for one person might not work for somebody else, coaching is all about empowering people to move forward by taking responsibility for their own decisions and actions.

This means asking questions which allow them to do this, inviting new perspectives and ways of thinking about challenges they may be seeking help on. We try to avoid asking closed questions with a 'yes' or 'no' answer, because this can close down conversations. Instead, we try to ask questions that start with, 'what', 'how', 'where', or 'when', for example.

These generally tend to work well for people with ADHD, who may give us lots of different answers in one - so it's important that we're actively listening and noticing what's being said. As a coach, I try to ask thoughtful questions and lead on with more, so even if my client has told me a super interesting tangent in between, I can bring them back to the focus of the session with my next question. In general, I suggest asking questions you can't easily guess the answer to!

5) Looking for the 'bright spots'

If you've met one person with ADHD, you've met one person with ADHD - we all have our unique systems and habits that work for us. The challenge for ADHD-ers is that these don't necessarily stay the same throughout our lives, because of our impacted executive functioning skills. I am great at starting new habits, but know I won't be able to sustain them.

In this way, coaching is a bit like being a detective. I am collaboratively working with my clients to help them understand what strategies work for them, and how to pick them back up again. We can take these strategies and make them fun and exciting again, re-energising us in returning to what we know will help us.

Coaching is great to help people remember the things that work for them and understand how they can apply these techniques to their present day. Asking 'what's worked before?' is a great reminder to draw upon our previous experiences - especially the challenges that we've overcome!

It can be very helpful to note these down in an ADHD Action Plan, as in chapter 'Creating an ADHD Friendly Culture', to support us with remembering what works as a visual reminder.

6) Acknowledging, accepting and validating people as they are

ADHD coaching can be an amazing experience in providing someone with the first shame-free space to be completely themselves - especially in a professional context. Every day, people tell me how incredible it is not to have to apologise for simply being themselves.

This shouldn't be such a rarity, but for people with ADHD who are used to masking themselves and second-guessing the things they're saying and doing, such as constantly apologising for interrupting or going off track, it often is. Having a space where we are accepted exactly as we are, in addition to being validated and supported by someone who isn't throwing advice and solutions at us in frustration, but simply saying 'I understand', is incredibly empowering.

This is what distinguishes ADHD coaching from neurotypical coaching. With the ADHD lens and knowledge of how it can show up, we understand how it's useless to tell someone with ADHD to simply 'try time management', or 'stop interrupting', for example. Believe me - if we could, we would have done it by now!

Instead, ADHD coaching tries a different method: meeting someone exactly where they are at, and helping them to move forward whilst being exactly who they are, instead of trying to force themselves to be different in some way. Understanding how our brain works means that we can stop beating ourselves up for being 'lazy' or 'stupid', for example, and start actually deciding what to do next in the ways that work for us. This starts with having the validation and acknowledgement from another human being that being who we are is okay, in allowing ourselves to truly be seen by another person.

Once we stop fighting against ourselves, the world becomes a lot easier to live in!

You don't need to be an 'official' ADHD coach to provide this type of support to someone, especially in the workplace. Taking these skills and applying them to your conversations can be powerful in and of itself.

Whether you are an individual with ADHD at work, a manager, or a HR professional, for example, having these coaching skills to hand can be very useful in navigating and harnessing ADHD at work. We can use them to help others (and ourselves!) understand how to get the most out of our environments, and ourselves, by identifying what works for us. You may find it helpful to use the example coaching scripts in this chapter when trying out using these skills.

I have/may have ADHD
Now what?

Here's an example script you can use
to help someone in this situation.

How do you feel?

'Thank you for sharing this with me - I imagine it may
be really overwhelming. How are you feeling?'

VALIDATE

Do you feel comfortable exploring this with me?

'There's no right or wrong answers, I'm here to
support you. How does this sound?'

REASSURE

What would you like to happen?

'I know you may not know, but what would be an ideal outcome from
this for you? In an ideal world, what would you like to happen?'

LISTEN

How can I help?

'If you'd like, I can help support you to explore your options.
Do you know about support like Access to Work?'

SIGNPOST

What support do you have in place?

'What's the first step you could take? How
can I help you put this into action?

FILTER

I'm struggling with ADHD
Can you help?

Here's an example script you can use to help someone in this situation.

Do you feel comfortable exploring this with me?

'Thank you for sharing this with me - I know how hard it can be to ask for help. I'm here to suport you with no judgement. How does that sound?'

REASSURE

What would be a good outcome?

'I don't expect you to have the answers, but what would you like to walk away with from today? How can I best support you?'

LISTEN

What are the challenges?

'What would you like to be different? What's worked before? What barriers are in your way? What steps do you need to take to do this? Did I understand this correctly?'

EXPLORE

How can I help?

'What support do you have in place? Would you like to explore creating an ADHD action plan? How do you feel about applying to Access to Work?'

SIGNPOST

What are you taking away from today?

'What SMART actions would you like to take from today? How can I help you to stay accountable?'

FILTER

Chapter 10
Managing ADHD For Success

As people with ADHD literally think differently to 'most' people, they are very different to manage in the workplace. Understanding ADHD empowers managers to provide a stimulating, effective workplace for people with ADHD, where they can thrive and utilise their unique thinking styles to reach their full potential at work. This benefits everybody!

What underlies this is the 'interest based nervous system' of an ADHD-er, compared to the 'importance based nervous system' of a neurotypical person. This is related to the 30% developmental delay in the executive functioning skill of motivation, which is linked with ADHD. In short, this means that people with ADHD are motivated differently than 'most' people, confusing the foundations of neuronormative management theory.

The concept of the interest based nervous system was coined by Dr William Dodson, who says that this means to do a task, a person must be 'personally interested, challenged, find it novel, or urgent right now, or nothing happens'. As Emily Katy says,[36] it's either 'I must do this *right now,* or procrastination.'

As a result, people with ADHD can be said to be motivated by novelty (a task being new and exciting), interest (personal to the individual), urgency, or challenge (such as a sense of competition).

In contrast, the average neurotypical brain is said to be 'importance based'. This means that they can do tasks according to the level of importance and priority (including to somebody else, rather than themselves), even if this isn't immediately urgent.

As a child, I was constantly asking 'why' I had to do things, with my innate ADHD curiosity questioning the status quo. I was often told, 'because I said so', which is probably the worst thing I could have been told, setting me up for a lifetime of challenging authority I didn't agree with! As an adult, this quality can be an amazing asset in the workplace, saving hours of inefficiencies that others may have simply become used to just because 'it's the way it is'.

At work, the role of a manager is ultimately to ensure that work gets done by the people who are supposed to be doing it. Traditional management styles may focus on 'importance based' motivational styles, highlighting prioritisation and clearly defined goals, but an

---

36 https://www.authenticallyemily.uk/blog/the-interest-based-nervous-system-and-adhd

ADHD-friendly one needs to account for the unique ways our brains work. Simply being given an arbitrary goal with zero context of meaning or purpose may not land with us as effectively as it would a neurotypical person. Often this may be for good reason, as this way of thinking can help to bring greater clarity and focus around work - but without tailored management styles and understanding, conflict may arise.

How to manage someone with ADHD

To manage a person with ADHD effectively, setting them up for success at work and harnessing their unique talents and ways of thinking, management styles simply need to be altered from the style of 'because I said so', to 'because you want to'.

In one job, I had to manage around 40 volunteers with no management training. I relied on the contributions of these volunteers to do my job effectively, but this was often a challenging thing to do, because their motivations could often be different to the organisation I was working for.

Luckily, my interest based nervous system brain enabled me to understand what uniquely motivated each of them, putting in the effort to ensure that each contribution they made was rewarding for them in some way and felt part of a collaborative team dynamic. I set clear expectations and transparency in what would happen thereafter, but motivated them to do their part by simply caring about connecting this to their wider motivation of volunteering in the first place.

A few months into the role, I attended a management training session in the hope that I'd learn some 'official' styles of management. I was surprised to find that all of these techniques such as 'prioritising' and 'time management' were based on the fact that people **had** to do the work because of the hierarchy of management.

I asked the trainers for tips to manage people who weren't obliged to do their job as volunteers, and was simply told that this wasn't covered in the session and they didn't know what to advise. I couldn't believe it!

This is part of what makes people with ADHD great managers, because we understand how to *engage* people. The compassion and motivation that accompanies ADHD, in addition to having interest based nervous systems ourselves, means that we inherently understand that the worst way to get someone to do something is because we tell them to do it.

Here are some management strategies to manage people with ADHD (and those without it - but maybe I'm just biased!):
1) Understand who you are managing and what they really want
As everybody is motivated differently, with unique interests and desires, it's important to understand

what drives an individual's motivation. Contrary to popular belief, not everybody is motivated by job titles and money. As an ADHD Coach, I am privileged to hear a huge range of dreams - from learning a new language and moving country, to learning a new skill or writing a book. They are endless.

One tool that may be helpful is a free strengths quiz from a website called VIA Character.[37] This helps with self-awareness, in understanding what a person's unique character traits are that make them feel best when they're being used. My top ones are creativity and curiosity, so having a working environ-ment where I'm able to come up with ideas and put them into reality (like this book!), is key to ensuring I remain motivated at work.

As a manager, it's extremely helpful to look into this in detail with the people you manage, to under-stand what they'd like out of their career and day to day working environment. I personally masked my goals in 'professional' workplace settings such as development reviews, putting goals that I thought were expected of me, such as the desire to 'improve my teamwork skills'. Encouraging employees to set the goals they *actually* want, even if they aren't strict-ly related to their job, helps managers understand how to frame their work in the most helpful way to

37 https://www.viacharacter.org

them so they can achieve these - they shouldn't be expected to stay with the company forever!

For example, managers can identify opportunities for learning, creativity, collaboration, or anything else within the context of the working environment, making the purpose of work relevant in a wider context than 'because I said so'.

2) Create meaning and ownership

To truly engage employees you manage, understand what is *meaningful* to them. Once you understand their desires, then you can understand what they care about, and how to translate this into their daily work.

Impact can be hard to measure and translate in the majority of corporate working environments. I am often complimented for my ability to do a job that 'does good' (and financially survive at the same time!), but this doesn't mean that we all need to be helping people or the world to feel that we are creating our desired impact. There's a reason the person is in their job specifically, and meaning can come from anything.

From a Cleaner to a Managing Director of an organisation, every person is there for a reason. As a manager, you can try to understand what that reason is, what impact that person would like to have in the world and how this can relate back to their work.

For example, if a person is disconnected from the meaning of their work, such as sales of something they don't personally believe in, managers can help them to create their own meaning around this. This could look like the purpose of their job in that moment, such as learning skills setting them up for future opportunities connected to their passion, or implementing their ideas at work and seeing these become reality.

A very simple way managers can do this is to encourage and listen to ideas and feedback. They can explain the core meaning and values behind the work and mission of a company, and encourage employees to set their own meaning and values of their role there, recognising that these do not neces- sarily have to be the same - but they can co-exist alongside each other.

3) Set actionable, short-term expectations, and provide positive feedback

As seen in chapter 'Reasonable Adjustments for ADHD', using a briefing document for work can be extremely helpful to ensure everybody is on the same page - literally. This means setting out 'what' exactly is expected of someone with regards to their work, breaking this down into SMART goals. Making the timeframe of these goals as short as possible helps to break 'marathons into sprints', which makes them more relevant for an ADHD brain that can struggle to connect with the long term future.

Clearly setting out expectations is crucial to seeing results: people with ADHD may take things literally and be unsure how to prioritise work. Explaining what is most important to do first and why, and when they should stop (i.e the 'Measurable' part of the SMART goal!), is important to avoid burnout and preserve energy. Providing templates and examples can also be very helpful.

These actions and goals should be celebrated and acknowledged appropriately as they happen, providing lots of opportunities for positive feedback and recognition. This helps people to know that they are meeting what is expected of them, building their confidence and empowering them to do more of the same. For people with ADHD, regular positive feedback is the easiest way to counteract the stress of Rejection Sensitive Dysphoria, as we build confidence at work.

Unfortunately, this counteracts traditional man-agement styles which tend to focus on 'areas for improvement'. For example, managers may be hesitant around focusing heavily on positive feedback out of fear that this could 'stop someone from trying', but this is exactly the opposite of how an ADHD brain works, in my experience. If you want our full dedication, passion, and loyalty, tell us we're doing a good job!

Ideally, write down these expectations and goals for everybody to access in one place, such as a briefing document, along with any sign-off processes. Preparing for this in advance, such as by setting up review time or meetings in calendars at the start of new work helps everybody to stick to the plan!

4) Use the 'interest based nervous system' to add motivation

Understanding the interest based nervous system means that work can be tailored to factor in interest, novelty, challenge and urgency as needed. This might look like providing shorter timeframes for certain work, or inviting feedback and ideas on how to make it more novel or interesting.

There are boring parts of every job, which can be especially difficult for people with ADHD to complete. Supporting them to identify these at the outset and 'hack' their motivation around them empowers them to implement strategies and skills to 'do what they know'. Approaching this with curiosity and creativity empowers people with ADHD to try out different strategies to see what works for them, resulting in a greater sense of ownership over their work. For example, they may wish to try out body doubling, task swapping, artificial deadlines, or extra accountability in confirming 'boring' tasks have been completed. The possibilities are endless - and they will have a wealth of ideas!

5) Provide a container for work to happen - and trust it to happen!

Trust is the single most important part of management. Providing structures for work to happen with systems such as a direct line in case of support that is needed, and/or relevant adjustments such as flexible working styles, is important to establish secure foundations and expectations.

Then in most cases, and provided proper business controls and metrics are in place, it can be argued that the best productivity results will be obtained when a person is permitted to get on with their work in the ways that work for them, avoiding micromanagement. The importance of this notion of empowerment in management style has developed to a completely new level in the post-pandemic world, where working from home is a new norm. As a manager, this means we need to set up routines for ourselves to provide consistency and trust. I've coached managers who have ADHD and struggle with this, impulsively 'checking in' on how something is going and leaving 27 comments (ok - this includes me!), which can lead to confusion and hurt feelings from the individual who may feel undermined half way through completing their work.

It's important that as managers, we can stick to our own expectations and remember these. For example, if we set a deadline for something, we should try our best to avoid chasing people before that deadline - which again, can be tough if we have ADHD ourselves. Setting up reminders, such as on a calendar, can be helpful for us to refocus our attention on ourselves and provide support when needed.

Ultimately, this means that to most effectively trust others, we should trust ourselves. Trusting people to get on with the job empowers them with autonomy and space to fail and learn from mistakes, with managers as supportive enablers.

6) Encourage communication and asking for help

Within this container for people to complete their work, there should be clearly defined and accessible lines of communication and trust. This could be systemised, such as regular 1:1 meetings where work (and workload!) can be reviewed to build confidence, ask questions, and receive feedback, or more ad hoc.

One manager we interviewed said this was one of the best adjustments she'd made, in simply replying to any questions from her employee with ADHD quickly via chat (as opposed to from others who she may have responded to later). Resolving small queries quickly and positively can be hugely beneficial to people with ADHD who may have a tendency to 'sweat the small stuff'.

We may also struggle with Rejection Sensitive Dysphoria and feel 'guilty' for asking for help, so consistently reminding them that this is a quality highly valued at work, and that asking for help helps everybody, is highly recommended. We may need to be reminded that asking for help means we are **good** at our jobs - not bad at them - and nobody knows everything!

7) Provide opportunities for ideas

One distinguishing feature of people with ADHD I've noticed in myself and others is that our brains are ideas-machines. As we are more energetic about the things we're interested in, we may have lots of brilliant ideas and feedback, which may not always be practical for a manager who's mainly concerned with getting the job done.

Knocking these ideas down can lead us to disengage and experience Rejection Sensitive Dysphoria, so providing boundaries and frameworks for ideas and feedback to be shared can be a healthy and highly beneficial balance. For example, having a 'blue sky thinking' day one per month, where people can present their ideas and take ownership for making them happen, can facilitate innovation and improvements in a sustainable and fair way for everybody.

Here are some management strategies to manage yourself and others if you have ADHD:

1) Be clear on what you're doing and why

Managing ourselves with ADHD can be challenging if we have lots of different goals and objectives. Being clearly aligned to our goals and motives, and embracing opportunities to make the most of our unique character strengths on a day to day basis, empowers us to lead the way for others.

Understanding our unique strengths and challenges is important for us to be able to delegate effectively. Knowing where our 80% 'zone of genius' lies enables us to ask for help for the more troublesome 20%.

2) Set clear SMART goals for others: who, what, and when!

Once we're clear on our own objectives, we can delegate out to others and support them at work. Setting out SMART goals enables us to think through what we're delegating more fully, establishing when precisely something would be finished, and helping us to set specific instructions. It can be easy to assume that everyone else has as whizzy brains as ours, but most people don't - and they need the full explanation of what they need to do.

Having a clear foundation of training set up can support people to learn what we mean. At ADHD Works, we have various resources and 'playbooks', enabling anybody new to the company to understand our standard operating procedures. This saves me from having to explain things repeatedly.

Setting these goals out clearly, and ensuring everybody understands exactly what they have to do, who is involved, and when it needs to be done by, empowers everyone to work together in a collaborative and organised way.

3) Set boundaries for yourself and others

As a manager, you are setting an example for your team. Filling up your own oxygen tank first enables you to demonstrate the importance of this for others and support everybody to avoid burnout. This also means saying no where needed, and setting boundaries such as specified working hours.

Personally, I can find this difficult to maintain, especially as I am often forgetting the boundaries I set! Having reminders up on my wall serve as important visual reminders. So even if I'm working on the weekend and want to reply to an email at 7pm on a Saturday night, seeing these reminders will help me to schedule the email to be sent at 9am on Monday. Although I could include a disclaimer about how I don't expect a reply, I know from personal experience that others may still feel tempted to reply during their time off.

4) Be vulnerable and compassionate

Many managers I see struggle with vulnerability, because they feel they need to 'be in charge'. However, sharing their vulnerability and experiences with those they manage can help to facilitate a stronger and more empathetic working relationship.

People with ADHD may resonate with the feeling that their manager simply doesn't care about them, but the opposite is often true. I've seen mangers go the extra mile to 'protect' employees from needless stress, such as taking on conversations about ADHD to HR and avoiding discussing this with an individual until they have an answer. However, the individual doesn't necessarily know this - so going the extra mile to show that they're on the person's side can be extremely helpful.

I see this a lot in managers who have ADHD themselves, taking on the problems and stresses of the people they manage. It's okay to communicate that you don't have all of the answers, and to share what's going on behind the scenes. Vulnerability is not a sign of weakness: it's a sign of strength, in showing that nobody has to have all of the answers for every situation, and you're doing your best!

5) Ask for help!

It's important that managers - especially those with ADHD - access the help they need in addition to helping others. They are often caught in the middle between HR and employees, and understandably may experience a lot of pressure.

For example, a manager may wish to ask for additional management training if an employee discloses ADHD to them - or if they learn that they have ADHD themselves. Seek support where needed: you are not alone, and helping yourself will help others.

Briefing
Document

Using a document such as this to plan out work amongst colleagues can be extremely helpful. Feel free to use and adapt this template as may be helpful.

Date:

Overview

What is the scope and purpose of the work?
· Specifically, what needs to happen? · How will you know when this is done? · Is this achievable within the timeframe? · What is the the relevance of this to wider goals? i.e. what's the point / what will it enable you do do next? · What time frames are involved?

When will this happen? When can you book in check in calls to monitor progress (tip: schedule these in the diary now!)?

Key dates:

Event	Deadline

Who else needs to be involved? What are their roles and remit?

Person	Responsibility

Anything else?

Chapter 11
ADHD Career Growth

With the right environment, people with ADHD can advance in their career just like anybody else, thriving within organisations and achieving great success at work.

However, as success looks different to everybody, it's important to ensure that the foundations of their working environments are set up for long-term career success: for them to not simply survive, but to thrive.

People with ADHD are said to be 300% more likely to set up their own businesses,[38] which means that without providing opportunities tailored for people with ADHD to progress their careers within their organisation, there's a real risk of employers missing out on these exceptional strengths and skills.

As explained in chapter 'Spotting ADHD at Work', the differences in executive functioning skills such as self-awareness and memory may provide

---

38 https://chadd.org/wp-content/uploads/2018/06/ATTN_10_14_Challenge.pdf

challenges for people with ADHD to share their successes in the same way as their colleagues. As this lack of self-promotion could hold them back in their career progression, it's important to consider when thinking about harnessing ADHD at work.

There may be a number of reasons for this:

Struggling to explain what we do

The differences in self-awareness and problem solving that accompany ADHD mean we may struggle to explain how or why we have done what we have done, which can make it feel challenging to take responsibility for our successes. For example, I rarely think about or plan things out before doing them - I just do them!

This can be confusing when trying to explain to another person how to do the same thing, because our brains may not break down our work into natural steps that can be easily followed by others.

The neuronormative expectations of our society generally expect us to be able to 'show our working out', right from when we're taking exams in school. I always remember being told to show how I'd achieved a certain answer, but I couldn't - I didn't know how I'd done it!

Interviews can implicitly set these same expectations, asking us to explain how we've handled certain tasks or situations. I once had an interview at an organisation who use the STAR method for interviews. Interviewees should explain the 'situation' they had to deal with, the 'task' they were given to do, the 'action' they took, and the 'result' - what happend as a result of the action, and what they learned from the experience.

Despite writing out about 50 versions of these answers and plastering them all over my wall for the (remote) interview, I still couldn't answer it in this format. My brain simply doesn't work that way - I can explain the story around it, but not in this prescribed format. A reasonable adjustment that could have helped me is not marking me in accordance with this STAR method, for example.

For employers, this is highly relevant in all interviews, appraisals and promotion opportunities where a person is expected to explain 'their workings out'. For example, I met a woman who said that because she was aware of this tendency, she started writing down what she was doing as she was doing it, to help leave a repeatable path of how she actually does her job. This document has now been shared across the organisation she works at and used by countless people, not just as a strategy for them to do the same in their own careers, but to help them understand how to do their own jobs!

These kinds of innovative strategies are exactly the sorts of brilliant benefits a neurodivergent mind can bring to the workplace. Especially during induction and training periods, it would be hugely beneficial for everybody to have a blueprint of exactly how to do their jobs in the ways that work best, with tasks broken down, instead of being left to figure this out by themselves!

Creating regular opportunities for employees with ADHD to share and record their 'workings out' in the ways that work for them can be extremely helpful for their own career advancement, in addition to others.

Instead of expecting them to do this in an arbitrary and abstract way such as with a line on a Personal Development Review document, they could be encouraged to find their own methods, such as by recording audio notes or writing a guidebook for others! If you're an employee with ADHD reading this, please take this as your encouragement to do so - keep a record of your work, even if it doesn't feel relevant right now.

It's helpful to have a reminder to do this, and somebody to help us identify how we are developing, such as by noting the skills that we have gained as a result of certain projects. ADHD coaching can be extremely helpful for this, as we help people to identify their wins and how these can be used going forwards.

Having an interest based nervous system

As people with ADHD are differently motivated to neurotypical people, they may not plan their work in the same way. For example, I often 'trust my gut', and still do not have a formal business plan, which seems to be working pretty well for ADHD Works!

However, in an organisation, especially one with lots of employees, we may not have the luxury of choosing what work we do because 'we feel like it'. This being said, employees with ADHD may have lots of brilliant ideas and initiatives, which we may execute without a follow up plan in mind. For example, we may wish to set up an Employee Resource Group, which can be a brilliant way of bringing together lots of colleagues to support each other at work.

Without a 'plan' in mind, it can be hard to present this objectively important and impressive work as part of our future career advancement goals, for example. This means that we may not always make the most of the things we do, or think about them in a way that could bring us a personal benefit - but we should!

In my experience, people with ADHD tend to connect the dots looking backwards, making sense of our decisions in retrospect. This style of living and planning may disadvantage us in the workplace, where we may be expected to have clear career journeys mapped out in a similar way to our colleagues.

This may be exacerbated by our tendency to experience time as 'now' or 'not now', making it difficult for us to think ahead and envision our futures. For example, when I was asked about my future career plans in a past job, I said I was already in my dream job, and my goal was to remain in it for at least one year. When I was asked what I'd like to do after that, I didn't have an answer - I just wanted to stay in it forever, and I didn't know what other opportunities were available to me.

This could be misunderstood by employers as complacency, preventing us from being offered the same opportunities as our colleagues who can clearly set out what they want in the future from their work. We may also not realise what other job roles could include, as we may be less motivated by hierarchy than others - so it's important that employers explain the benefits and differences involved in potential job opportunities.

An example of this was when I was asked during an interview which other organisations I had applied to for a legal training contract. I answered honestly: none! I just really loved this one employer, and hyper-focused on this one instead of considering working elsewhere. I was told informally that this was a reason that I wasn't successful, because they didn't think I was serious about becoming a lawyer.

By understanding more about different ways of thinking, employers can adjust their practices to ensure that people with ADHD can thrive at work, and make the most of their talents. This could include providing mentoring or shadowing schemes, enabling people to try out new areas of work, and helping people to focus on their strengths and skills from the work they have done.

Providing opportunities for these to be put into practice is also very important, as in chapter 'Managing ADHD for Success'. Employees with ADHD may have a wide variety of interests and talents, and supporting them to use them, even if these fall outside of their prescribed job description, can benefit everybody.

Employers can also actively challenge their own biases, such as requiring a certain number of years' experience in a certain role or viewing career gaps or changes in a negative way. Staying in a job you don't like for a certain period of time doesn't make a person good at their job, and it's much better for employers to have truly engaged and effective employees who want to be there, than those who don't.

Hiring someone with this authentic mindset means you know they are giving their all to whatever it is that they're doing - otherwise they wouldn't be there! People with ADHD in particular may have lots of different job experiences which should be valued, as they will have lots of different transferable skills, and be able to easily adapt into a workplace. This is the benefit of us connecting the dots backwards!

As an individual with ADHD, I'd recommend embracing these parts of you, and remembering that they can and should be used to advance your career, even if it feels non-traditional. Having a coach or mentor can help you to make the most of these dots, and present them in a way that benefits your future, which you fully deserve!

Forgetting Our Successes

As people with ADHD may experience challenges with their short and long term memories, they may be prone to forgetting their successes as quickly as they achieve them! For example, I am constantly forgetting what I've written in the books I have written and published, so I can often feel like an imposter when people are referencing them back at me.

In an organisation, we may need to be our own cheerleader, drawing attention to our successes as much as our colleagues are able to do for themselves. Having a super quick, dopamine seeking brain means that as soon as we achieve something, we may 'move the goal posts' and set ourselves more and more to do before we can celebrate our success.

This means that we may not take responsibility or ownership for our strengths at work, which can lead other people to fill the gaps, even if we've done a lot of the work! It can also make us underplay our own successes, which is something I see a lot in my coaching clients.

As career reviews are often done periodically, such as every quarter or year, it's important for employees with ADHD to record their successes regularly in between this. Otherwise, it can be very difficult for us to remember and present our development in these meetings.

For example, they could record their 'weekly wins' each Friday afternoon, sharing these with a team. I always start coaching sessions by asking for a win of the week from my clients, which is a great way to build their memory and self-esteem by implementing the habit of recalling successes from their week. This is something that could be easily translated to the workplace, such as opening team meetings by asking everybody to share a win.

Employers can also provide systems for colleagues to support each other with celebrating their wins in a visible way. For example, in a previous job, employees could nominate their colleagues for a 'shout out' at department-wide meetings, which was a highly effective way to draw visibility to their work. Having 'nomination' style cards can also be very helpful, where colleagues can send each other tokens of appreciation or celebration for their work.

Again, this can be extremely helpful for everybody, fostering an engaged, supportive and appreciative culture amongst employees. Managers can take extra care to remind employees with ADHD to record, share, or celebrate their successes in the ways that work for them, including by providing positive feedback and noting these themselves!

For individuals with ADHD, I strongly recommend creating a 'wins' notebook, and noting down the things you've done or your achievements as regularly as you can remember, such as the start of every month. These don't have to be in any particular format or meet any criteria - you don't have to have written an entire report to be able to count it as a win!

If this feels awkward, you could start with a 'Have Done' list, noting down all of the things you've done at the end of the day - an opposite 'to do' list! Simply keeping track of the things we've done can help us to reflect on these and realise how much we're doing on a daily basis, which is probably a LOT!

Rejection Sensitive Dysphoria

As people with ADHD can experience challenges with regulating their emotions, Rejection Sensitive Dysphoria can significantly hold us back from advancing our careers.

Almost every single person I've coached has struggled with visibility, and the fears of being seen as 'difficult', 'arrogant', or 'too much' as they are. Growing up with ADHD in a world that is not tailored towards our needs can be extremely challenging and have a significant impact on our self-esteem. We may struggle with self-promotion and sharing our successes out of fear of upsetting other people, even minimising our efforts, yet actively celebrate others!

We may also be extremely honest and take things very literally, so if the requirements of a job role are vague, such as being a 'good communicator', we may not apply for this if we are not good at a certain aspect of communication, such as speaking on the telephone. It's important that job criteria is adapted accordingly to be as specific as possible, with a clear explanation that aspects can be made flexible and adapted as needed.

I have experienced this throughout my career, having panic attacks before interviews and quitting them completely out of anxiety. I genuinely believed I'd be told off somehow for tricking the interviewers! This also applied to my work, where I was often very nervous about making a mistake, and thinking this could lead to me being fired.

I was also very nervous about applying for any opportunities to progress my career in case I got in trouble, or my employer thought I wasn't committed to my current role. Getting the balance right between appearing ambitious and committed was extremely stressful to navigate, and led me to mask my anxiety, taking no action.

This intense fear of rejection may also result in people with ADHD avoiding situations where this could happen, such as by applying for a job, or asking for the help they need to do their job to the best of their abilities. I have coached many people who've all expressed the same anxiety around asking for help, in case the 'worst case scenario' happened and they would have to leave their job!

It may feel excruciating to interview for a job and not be accepted, but to have to remain in your current role. This can be alleviated by providing clear, transparent information about job roles, interview processes, and honest feedback.

It's extremely important for employers to ensure there is psychological safety for neurodivergent people at work, as in chapter 'Creating an ADHD Friendly Culture'. Having extra care taken out to help employees plan their career paths is important to ensure that they are using their full abilities at work, and remain engaged and loyal to their employer.

People with ADHD may also feel nervous about advancing their career if they cannot see any representation of people like them in these roles, which is why it's equally important for those in senior roles to be vulnerable and honest about their own experiences and challenges.

Employers can also tackle this by providing tailored mentorship and coaching programmes, in addition to 'champions' schemes where employees could help to celebrate and encourage each other.

As an individual, it's important to remember that you need to share your wins, and you deserve to grow and thrive within your work! By contributing your full efforts and talents with your employer, you are helping them, and by sharing your successes with your colleagues, you are empowering others to do the same. It can feel safer to stay where you are, but your ADHD brain thrives on stimulation, so don't be afraid to stand out, embrace your differences, and go for all of the things that you want to do.

Redefining 'Success'

It's important to consider making reasonable adjustments in the context of a person's future career, as well as the disadvantages they may be experiencing at a particular point in time. This involves thinking about how to adjust career paths to make them accessible and inclusive to a range of people. It's also a great opportunity for employers to reevaluate what 'success' looks like, and what they value within their employees at an organisation-wide level.

For example, my background is in the legal industry, which traditionally operates on a 'billable hours' basis of success. The performance of solicitors tends to be evaluated on how many client hours they bill, which in my opinion, is outdated for the current world we live in, leaving the industry open to disruption, for example.

In my experience, this system doesn't work for anyone. From the clients who are uncertain about how many hours they will be charged, and understandably feel nervous about large legal fees being racked up without their knowledge, to the solicitors who have to work in ways that may not feel as efficient as they could be, this system slows everybody down. It was incredible to find a solicitor called Sam Walkley,[39] who offered fixed and highly affordable fees, regardless of how much additional back and forth would be needed.

This is exactly the kind of service that is likely to disrupt and undercut traditional law firms if they do not adapt to what their clients need, especially as technological advancements such as ChatGPT can create a contract in seconds (though not necessarily with the same credibility or accuracy!).

A system of billable hours is *especially* unlikely to work for lawyers with ADHD. I've worked with several who have had significant issues arising from doing a huge amount of work, but forgetting to record it as needed. These repetitive, administrative tasks can be very challenging for people with ADHD, especially when they're used to working in highly stimulating and adrenaline-filled environments. We can also do a huge amount of work very quickly, which might result in us doing more work, but for less money or recognition than our colleagues, which ultimately defeats the point!

---

39 http://www.xvolegal.co.uk/

Continually reassessing how success is measured is important for any organisation to do, to ensure they are working effectively. Setting SMART targets that are tangibly and clearly aligned with company goals enables everybody to engage in pursuit of a common purpose, as opposed to being held to arbitrary and disconnected objectives for the sake of it.

As in chapter 'Managing ADHD for Success', ensuring that ADHD employees understand the *why* behind their work enables them to activate their interest based nervous systems to perform to the best of their abilities.

Encouraging them to redefine what success looks like for themselves and to set goals in accordance with this is highly empowering, and likely to result in happier, loyal, and engaged employees. Criteria for progression and promotion can be adapted to meet these goals - not everybody wants to be the CEO!

Template:
Personal Development Plan

As people with ADHD can struggle when thinking about the future, helping them to create their own personal development 'bucket list' career plan is a helpful way for them to set goals and work backwards.

Personal development
Plan

Make each section connect to the relevant SMART goal:

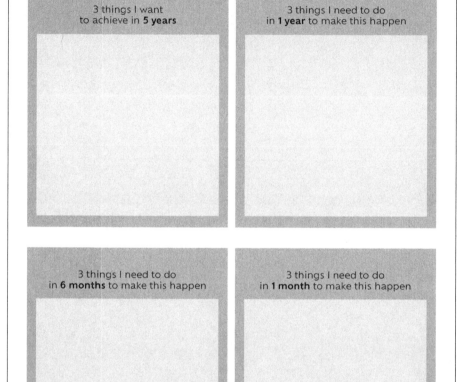

3 things I want
to achieve in **5 years**

3 things I need to do
in **1 year** to make this happen

3 things I need to do
in **6 months** to make this happen

3 things I need to do
in **1 month** to make this happen

Printed in Great Britain
by Amazon

47786386R00139